MW01284064

DRAWING OUT
MOSES AND OLD TESTAMENT LAW

ERIC WALLACE and NATHAN LEE

ONESTONE
BIBLICAL RESOURCES

Published by:
One Stone Press
979 Lovers Lane
Bowling Green, KY 42103

Printed in the United States of America

ISBN 10: 1-941422-25-X
ISBN 13: 978-1-941422-25-0

Supplemental Materials Available:

➢ Answer Key

➢ Downloadable PDF

ONE STONE
BIBLICAL RESOURCES

1(800)428-0121
www.onestone.com

INTRODUCTION

In one of the most ironic of circumstances, a man who was raised in the leader of Egypt's household will forsake what could have been a life of prestige and instead lead his native people against their biggest enemy... the leader of Egypt. That man is Moses. Not only will he go on to save his people from the Egyptians, he will be a central character in several Old Testament books (Exodus, Leviticus, Numbers, and Deuteronomy) that contain the detailed history of the Israelites, their journeys, and their divine law prescribed by God. DRAWING OUT attempts to draw out milestone events and concepts in an effort to provide the reader with the background, context, and importance of the Old Testament Law and surrounding narratives throughout the life of Moses.

DRAWING OUT – which gets its name from the Hebrew definition of Moses – has been designed to engage the student and spark discussion and application of Old Testament examples, principles, and characters.

Each of the 24 lessons is designed to draw out...

      ...the highlights and major events

      ...the context and summary of the biblical text

      ...deeper meanings and powerful concepts

      ...applications to Christians in today's world

      ...thought questions and classroom discussion

TABLE OF CONTENTS

LESSON ONE
MEET MOSES
Exodus 1-2

DRAWING OUT **HIGHLIGHTS**

- The Israelite nation is in the midst of Egyptian slavery
- Moses is born – and lives – despite a ruling to kill infant sons
- Moses is raised by Pharaoh's daughter and becomes her son
- Moses kills an Egyptian who is beating a fellow Hebrew
- Moses flees to Midian for forty years and finds a wife
- God hears the Israelites' cry to release them from their slavery

DRAWING OUT **CONTEXT**

Before we meet Moses, it's important to understand the situation of the Israelites when Moses appears on the scene. Years after Joseph was sold into slavery, Joseph settled in Egypt, his family joined him, and the Israelite people grew in number. New leadership in Egypt saw this growing number of Hebrews as a possible threat to their nation [1:9-14]. While the Israelite people had been forced into hard labor and worked as slaves for many years, male infants were ordered to be killed at the hands of midwives to stop their growing number [1:15f]. When that didn't work, Pharaoh ordered the Israelites to throw their newborn sons into the Nile river – killing them [1:22]. Moses was one of those newborns and was indeed thrown into the river, but survived inside a basket. Pharaoh's daughter found Moses and, even knowing he was one of the Hebrews' children, took the child for her own and named him 'Moses' because he was drawn out of the water [2:1-10].

Moses was raised in royalty, educated, and well-versed in the Egyptian culture and ways of life. However, Moses was still a Hebrew. When he was forty years old, he witnessed an Egyptian attacking a fellow Hebrew and killed the Egyptian [2:11f]. Even though Moses had lived as a privileged Egyptian, he had still committed a heinous crime. Moses initially thought no one was aware of what had happened. When he learned that others (as well as Pharaoh) were aware of his crime, he left Egypt and fled to Midian [2:13-15]. While in Midian, Moses found a wife, Zipporah, and had a son named Gershom [2:21f]. He remained in the Sinai desert for forty years.

Meanwhile, back in Egypt, the Israelites had more than they could take and began crying out to God. God heard their cry and remembered (i.e., took action on) his promises to Abraham, setting a plan in motion to remove their burden of slavery [2:23-25].

DRAWING OUT **DEEPER MEANINGS**

Moses Was Highly Educated

While we think of typical slaves in captivity as being uneducated, we sometimes forget that Moses was exposed to probably "the best education money could buy" as the son of the Pharaoh's daughter. Not only would this have been a read-and-write kind of education, but most likely one that also included military training, or even military command training... which may have served this future leader of the Israelite people well one day.

Moses Acted "By Faith"

Hebrews 11:24-27 tells us that Moses had great faith in God well before God called him at the burning bush. He first chose to be with his own/ God's people (instead of the Egyptians) "by faith." Then, after killing the Egyptian, he left Egypt "by faith" (not out of fear of Pharaoh). This faith in God certainly didn't come from Pharaoh's daughter, but was probably developed before he was three or four years old by his birth mother and/ or family, before Pharaoh's daughter took him to be her own.

"Remembering" and "Forgetting" in the Bible

We read in Exodus 2:24 that God "remembered" His promises to Abraham, but it's important to note that it does not mean God had forgotten about them. To "remember" in the Bible means to take action and do something about it. Similarly, when we read that the Israelites "forgot" God (cf. Judges 3:7) it does not mean they didn't remember who God was, but instead that they did not take action with or for God – they neglected Him.

DRAWING OUT **TAKE AWAYS**

Three things you should remember after reviewing this lesson:

1. God Can Use Anyone

Moses was supposed to be dead. Moses grew up in a pagan environment. Moses killed a man. Moses this, Moses that—the list goes on as we continue to read about this man. Moses was the one that God chose to set His people free and lead them to new lands and laws. God chose a murderer to do that. Let that sink in. God can use anyone for His purpose, and we must never think that we've done something too unforgivable or that God cannot use "me;" Moses was living proof to the contrary.

2. Sin is a Passing Pleasure

Hebrews 11:24-27 tells us that Moses chose to forgo the "passing pleasures of sin" and rather chose to "suffer affliction" with God's people. What an insight the Hebrew writer gives us into Moses and his actions. In his position, he could have had it all. But he chose not to because he knew those were passing pleasures and looked to a greater reward. What a reminder for us when we're in similar situations – to keep our eyes on the goal of pleasing God, even when the pleasures of sin may be thrown in our laps.

3. Don't Forget About God

Spending hundreds of years in Egypt may have caused the Israelite people to forget about God or caused them to put their trust in Egypt's gods.

It might have made sense to an Israelite; Egypt's gods must be more powerful because their own God (Jehovah) was keeping them in slavery! For us, we need to remember that God is always in control and never forget about Him or turn to other "gods" in trying times, even when we feel God isn't helping our situation. It was only when the Israelites truly called upon God to help them that He listened and responded.

DRAWING OUT **THOUGHT QUESTIONS**

1. How did the Israelites end up in Egypt and why was Pharaoh threatened

   by them? _____

   _____

   _____

   _____

2. What is the irony in Pharaoh's decree regarding infant Hebrew sons

   and the tenth plague that Pharaoh and the Egyptians faced? _____

   _____

   _____

   _____

   _____

3. How did Moses' sister play a role in him not being killed or left afloat?

   _____

   _____

   _____

   _____

   _____

4. If Moses was raised as Pharaoh's daughter's son, how did he know about the true God vs. the gods of Egypt? _____

_____

_____

_____

_____

5. Acts 7:23-25 gives us insight into Moses and his killing of the Egyptian. What was Moses thinking and why? _____

_____

_____

_____

_____

LESSON TWO

WHO AM I?

Exodus 3-4

DRAWING OUT **HIGHLIGHTS**

- God calls out to Moses through a burning bush on Mount Sinai
- Moses asks God a series of questions in which God responds
- Moses prepares to leave Midian for Egypt with his family and Aaron
- God prepares Moses by telling him what to do in front of Pharaoh
- God seeks to kill Moses on the journey to Egypt, but Zipporah saves Moses' life

DRAWING OUT **CONTEXT**

Moses, now about eighty years old and a shepherd for his father-in-law Jethro, or Reuel [2:18], was shepherding the flock one day near Mount Horeb, otherwise known as Mount Sinai. All of a sudden, the angel of the Lord appeared to him in a blazing fire from the midst of a bush [3:1-3]. From this burning bush God called out to Moses, and Moses responded with "Here am I!" Being in the presence of the Lord caused the ground to become holy, which prompted Moses to remove his sandals and hide his face in his cloak. God proceeded to give a message of compassion, saying how He remembers and cares for His people...so much that He will bring them out of Egypt into a land flowing of milk and honey. However, there were already groups of people occupying that land (the Canaanites, Hittites, Amorites, Perizzites, Hivites, and Jebusites). Yet the assurance God gave Moses of "I will be with you" [3:11-12] should have given God's people all the confidence in the world.

God commissioned Moses to a very important task – to stand in front of Pharaoh and bring God's children out of Egypt [3:10]. At this point in the conversation, Moses asked God a series of questions [3:11-4:16]. In summary, God told Moses all the things that would happen to him. Moses served a God who had a specific plan for the future of His people. After the conversation with God, Moses prepared to leave Midian for good, taking his family and the staff of God with him. This staff, God says, is the means by which signs will happen in front of Pharaoh [4:17]. Moses met with Aaron and relayed to Aaron all that God had told him on the mountain. Before arriving in Egypt, God sought to kill Moses because Moses did not circumcise his son. Moses' wife, Zipporah, intervened and took matters into her own hands by circumcising her son for Moses, sparing him from the wrath of God. At last, Moses and his family arrived in Egypt and met with the leaders of the Israelites, who praised God for their upcoming salvation from the Egyptians.

DRAWING OUT **DEEPER MEANINGS**

Identity of the Angel of the Lord

There are a number of times in scripture where we see angels taking a more active role. Often times it is clear that angels are simply angels, being described as "an" angel of the Lord (cf. Acts 5:19). But in other contexts, an angel seems to take on the identity of God Himself, being described as "the" angel of the Lord (cf. Judges 2:1). In Exodus 3, the title "the angel" is used in verse two, but the title is then switched in verse four to "God." This angel is speaking in the place of God and perfectly represents the Lord in this context.

Humble Objections or Lazy Excuses?

In chapters three and four, Moses asks God questions to which God responds with various answers. Some Bible students think Moses is offering up a series of excuses to God, while other Bible students think Moses is offering up a series of legitimate concerns. Notice a few things about these exchanges:

• Moses is bold enough to speak his mind to God and cast all cares and anxieties upon Him (cf. 1 Pet 5:7).

• God's response is one of patience and reassurance; not because of Moses' talent, but of God's ability to provide and lead Moses.

• Moses, although humble, is wrongly hesitant even after being consoled by the words and power of God [4:13].

I Am Who I Am

There are many names for God in the Bible and all of them carry some special significance, but none carry as much significance as the name "I am." This name, used in Exodus 3:14, is composed of four Hebrew consonants: YHWH. English versions of the Bible almost always translate the Hebrew consonants YHWH as "LORD" (with all capital letters). The Bible uses the name "I am" or YHWH as the ultimate name of God (the most holy of holy names) and places special significance to it directly [3:15]. So whenever we hear the name Yahweh, see the name "I am," or read the name LORD, we are talking about the same God by using the most special name He ever gave to His people. Understanding this name gives greater meaning to Christ's proclamation in Mark 14:62 that Jesus is "I am."

DRAWING OUT **TAKE AWAYS**

Three things you should remember after reviewing this lesson:

1. God Cares About His People

Many people in the world think God has forgotten them and that He does not care for them. In a world of pain and suffering, many wonder if God even cares about the world anymore. This is a parallel to the Israelites, who were probably asking themselves the same questions while in Egyptian bondage. Yet God says to Moses that He is still the God who spoke to Abraham, Isaac, and Jacob [3:6]. God says to Moses that He has heard the cries of the Israelites [3:7] and God says to Moses that salvation is coming soon [3:8]. When we feel that God does not care about us, remember He is still the same God (Heb 13:8), He hears our cries (1 John 5:14) and He provides salvation for all who come to Him (Acts 4:12).

2. God Can Use You, No Matter Who You Are

Moses asks God, "Who am I?" This is a legitimate concern and question that we should all ask ourselves. The humble hearted person is one who will look at self and realize their unworthiness compared to a holy God. Without God, we are nothing and we cannot stand (cf. Rev 6:17). Moses had a self-realization of this humbled state. Yet we cannot stop there. The mistake Moses made was not in asking "Who am I?" but rather not realizing that God can take the most unqualified, undeserving individuals and use them for His glory. We need to humbly accept that it is God working in us and let it motivate us to boldly proclaim, "Here am I! Send me!" (Isaiah 6:8).

3. God Expects Obedience

The Israelites have a historical 'problem' of committing sins right after experiencing God's glory on a mountain. For example, Moses and Zipporah [4:24-26] and Aaron with the golden calf in Exodus 32 all commit sins. Although it might seem like a small thing to not circumcise your child, to create a golden image, or to eat a small piece of fruit in the garden, etc., God expects you to obey Him in all matters of life. Moses could not be a physical leader of the people without being a good spiritual leader. For us, we need to obey God in all things, so we can become spiritual leaders for His kingdom.

DRAWING OUT **THOUGHT QUESTIONS**

1. Why did God have Moses take off his shoes? Are there any other groups of people in the Bible that God told to take off their shoes? _____

   _____

   _____

2. Was Moses right or wrong in asking God a series of questions? ____

_____

_____

_____

3. At what point did God get mad at Moses on Mount Sinai and why did He get mad? _____

_____

_____

_____

4. Who are some other characters in the Bible whom God used for a specific purpose? _____

_____

_____

_____

5. What are some specific circumstances in life where we might be tempted to not obey God? _____

_____

_____

_____

LESSON THREE

MORE WORK FOR THE WEARY

Exodus 5-7:13

DRAWING OUT **HIGHLIGHTS**

- Pharaoh denies Moses' request to let God's people go
- Pharaoh worsens the Israelites' workload in response
- The people blame Moses and Aaron for their continued hardship
- God reassures Moses He will deliver His people from the Egyptians
- Moses and Aaron perform a miracle in front of Pharaoh
- Pharaoh's heart is hardened and he refuses to let God's people go

DRAWING OUT **CONTEXT**

Moses and Aaron requested that Pharaoh allow the Israelites to hold a festival for the Lord in the wilderness, away from their work. Pharaoh declined their request and asked who is "this Lord" that is making such a request. Upset, he increased the Israelites' workload by making them find their own straw to make bricks – which added more time and effort – yet requiring the same number of bricks to be made [5:1-14]. When the people questioned Pharaoh, he responded by saying the Israelites are lazy and they always want to go and "sacrifice to the Lord." Realizing Pharaoh was upset and their increased workload continued to be enforced, the leaders went to Moses and Aaron and blamed them for what had happened [5:15-21].

Moses turned to God and asked for an explanation. God responded and said He would indeed set the Israelites free and possess them as His people. But when Moses relayed to the Israelites what God told him, the people did not want to hear it [6:1-9]. Departing briefly from the narrative, the genealogical record of Moses and Aaron is listed in verses 14-25 for the purpose of showing Moses' and Aaron's lineage.

After God instructed Moses (who is eighty years old) to tell Pharaoh to release the people again, Moses said that he was not the best speaker for the job, so God told Moses to have Aaron speak to Pharaoh. God informed Moses that Pharaoh would not listen to them, however, and that his heart would be hardened. But later, after signs and wonders, the Israelites would be released and Pharaoh, along with all the Egyptians, would truly know who God is [7:1-5].

When they finally approached Pharaoh, God told them to perform a miracle of turning Aaron's staff into a snake. After seeing the miracle performed, Pharaoh called his magicians and they too turned their staffs into snakes. However, Aaron's staff swallowed up the magicians' staffs and Pharaoh's heart was then hardened [7:8-12]. What came next was a series of signs and wonders that further demonstrated God's awesome power.

DRAWING OUT **DEEPER MEANINGS**

Hardening Pharaoh's Heart

Did God force Pharaoh to not let the Israelites go by hardening his heart? It may seem to some that God was forcing Pharaoh to do something against his will. It's clear that Pharaoh – on his own, with no influence from God – would not have simply allowed the entire Israelite population to leave because Moses asked. There was no reason or incentive for him to do so. Furthermore, if God was forcing Pharaoh to do something he didn't want to do by hardening his heart, it would have been against his will; we know God does not operate like that and He does not force anyone to do anything against his or her own free will. The Egyptians had many gods including Re (the god of the sun) which was one of the "great gods." The Pharaohs were also considered to be gods and actual descendants of Re themselves. If Pharaoh regarded himself as a god, we can see why Moses' continued requests coming from "the God of Israel" would have been so offensive. Pharaoh didn't continue to act the way he acted because of God forcing him to do so through the hardening of his heart. Pharaoh acted the way he did and was the kind of person he was by his own nature. In reality, all God had to do to harden his heart was to show more of Himself to Pharaoh, allowing all the people to see how He is the true God and how Pharaoh wasn't a god at all. Pharaoh would simply not believe...by no fault (or force) of God.

Knowing God's Name

God said to Moses in Exodus 6:3 that He did not make His name known to Abraham, Isaac, and Jacob (i.e., the patriarchs of the past). But did that mean they did not know God's name? Certainly not. When we read that a name is "made known" in the Bible, that means the people experienced the attributes, actions, and personality of the person – not simply his or her name. In the narrative, God didn't make His name known in the past to the degree that He was going to do so now. God demonstrated His all-powerful attributes, abilities, and personality when He took action against the Egyptians. At that point, His name would be made better-known through His acts. The Israelites (and Pharaoh) knew that the Lord was the one who was responsible for what was going to happen, but at this point He was only a name. After the Lord demonstrated His power, His character, and they experienced who He is, they would know fully what His name means. One can "know of" someone and one can "know" someone – two very different things.

Egyptian Magic

It is clear in the text that the Egyptian magicians were able to turn their staffs into snakes. But how? While we are not completely sure, the Bible demonstrates in passages such as 2 Thessalonians 2:9, Matthew 24:24, and in the book of Revelation that demons had the power to perform signs and wonders. If that was the case in Moses' day, then the magicians could have been able to perform the same sign Aaron did, not by the power of God, but by the power of demons. If the sign was not performed by the power of supernatural beings, it simply could have been performed like a magic trick is performed today – fooling the spectators into thinking something happened that really did not. In either case, we see that God's signs and wonders undoubtedly prove to everyone that He is not simply performing a magic trick or an illusion, but that His miracles are far above anything man or other supernatural beings can do.

DRAWING OUT **TAKE AWAYS**

Three things you should remember after reviewing this lesson:

1. The Old Testament Shows Us Who God Is

While understanding that Christians are not under the Old Testament laws, some beg the question of the need to study the Old Testament, especially the books of law. Through the laws and narratives contained therein (and in other sections throughout Old Testament) one can really "get to know" God. God told Moses that until this time others before Him didn't truly know His name (i.e., His character.) But studying the Old Testament and law books shows us who God is – His character, His power, how humans are imperfect, how His chosen people do not always follow Him, and how He deals with them throughout history. Without the Old Testament and only the information we have in the New Testament, we too might be like those before Moses who knew of God, but didn't get the chance to really know and understand who He is.

2. Don't Give Up in Times of Disappointment

The Israelites had a tough time. After Moses spoke to Pharaoh and requested they be allowed to leave, times got even tougher. What a disappointment to the Israelite people who were told God would save them! After Pharaoh's new work mandate we see a contrast in how Moses and the Israelites dealt with this blow. The people acted in disbelief because their situation worsened. Moses, on the other hand, acted in faith and continued to trust in God and ask for their deliverance. When we experience hard times in our lives we need to trust in God. A situation might get worse before it gets better and things may be happening for reasons that don't make sense to us at the time (cf. Joseph in Genesis 50:20). Christians are not exempt from troublesome times, but with faith in God, they can get through any rough patch that may befall them.

3. Knowledge of God is Polarizing

The more one knows God, the more polarizing He becomes. One will either accept Him or deny Him. Like Pharaoh, our hearts are either hardened as clay in the sun (i.e., we push away from God and resist Him) or our hearts are melted like wax in the sun (i.e., we accept God and yield to Him). It's the same sun, but two very different results. It's the same God, but two very different reactions. When the people learned more about Jesus in Peter's first sermon in Acts 2, the people were so struck by what they heard that they had a decision to make – be humble and ask what they can do to be in good standing with God or revolt against Peter and deny God's Son, pushing Him away. When we learn more or teach the gospel to others, it does the same: melts or hardens hearts. That's the power of God and His message (cf. Heb 4:12).

DRAWING OUT **THOUGHT QUESTIONS**

1. Contrast the difference in attitudes Moses and the Israelites had after Pharaoh increased their workload. _____

_____

_____

_____

2. Knowing what we know about Pharaoh, would he have let the Israelites go if God had not hardened his heart? Why? _____

_____

_____

_____

3. Why do the genealogies listed in Exodus 6:13-25 "suddenly appear" in the middle of the narrative? What purpose do they serve and why were they important to readers? _____

_____

_____

_____

4. How do the parables of Jesus demonstrate the polarizing nature of God, His will, and His teachings to people listening to them in Jesus' day? __

_____

_____

_____

5. Besides learning more about God's character as seen in the Old Testament, what other benefits are there to studying the Old Testament and Old Testament laws? _____

_____

_____

_____

LESSON FOUR
LET MY PEOPLE GO!
Exodus 7:14-10:29

DRAWING OUT **HIGHLIGHTS**

• In an effort to get Pharaoh to let God's people leave, God sends nine plagues upon Egypt, all of them eliciting a stubborn response of refusal from Pharaoh
• Each plague shows God's power to His own people, to Pharaoh, and to prove His dominance when compared to Egyptian gods

DRAWING OUT **CONTEXT**

Even though God clearly showed His power over Pharaoh by Aaron's staff turning into a snake, Pharaoh had a stubborn heart and did not listen to Moses and Aaron. What happened next was a series of signs and wonders that can only be described as miracles from God. These were not natural wonders that just so happened to occur, but rather clear and intentional messages and plagues from God. We have nine plagues recorded for us:

1. Water to Blood [7:14-25]

The Nile River was not just any body of water, it was the lifeblood of Egypt. It was so important to Egypt that they held a claim of ownership to the river (Ezek 29:9). The Nile turning into blood was not just a "slap in the face" to Egypt, but possibly to their river gods Khnum (guardian of Nile's source), Hapi (spirit of the Nile), and Osiris (his bloodstream was the Nile). This plague affected both Egypt and Goshen (where the Israelites lived), was duplicated by the Egyptian magicians, and caused the fish to die/rot in the waters.

2. Frogs [8:1-15]

The plague of frogs could possibly be seen as a counterpart to the Egyptian gods Hapi and Heqt, who were frog goddesses related to fertility. Pharaoh asked the frogs to leave Egypt and promised to let the Israelites leave to worship. But Pharaoh broke his promise after Moses prayed to God for the frogs to be removed. The frogs died and rotted across the lands of Egypt and Goshen. Egyptian magicians were also able to duplicate this plague to some extent.

3. Gnats [8:16-19]

Also called lice, this plague might have showed God's power over the Egyptian god Seb (the earth god of Egypt). The Egyptian magicians could not find a way to duplicate this plague; they could only credit the plague to the "finger of God" [8:19].

4. Flies or Insects [8:20-32]

From this point forward, the plagues did not affect Goshen but only Egypt. These flies were probably more than just houseflies, but rather large insects that swarmed both homes and lands. This plague could possibly be a contrast to the Egyptian god Uatchit (the fly god of Egypt).

5. Death of Livestock [9:1-7]

There were a few Egyptian gods that were associated with cows: Ptah, Hathor, Mnevis, and Amon. This plague affected property of Egyptian individuals by killing horses, donkeys, camels, cows, and sheep.

6. Boils [9:8-12]

The boils could be interpreted in varying degrees of physical ailments, but we know for certain that it was so bad the magicians could not even stand or appear in court. God might have showed His power through boils over the Egyptian gods Sekhmet (goddess of Epidemics) and/or Serapis and Imhotep (Egyptian gods of healing).

7. Hailstorm [9:13-35]

God sent storms like Egypt had never seen before as a possible contrast to the Egyptian gods Nut (sky goddess), Isis and Set (agriculture deities), and Shu (god of the atmosphere). Pharaoh admitted to having sinned during this plague and promised to let the people go, but after the hail stopped, Pharaoh broke his promise yet again.

8. Locusts [10:1-20]

In bringing to mind Serapia (the Egyptian locusts deity protector), God sent locusts to devour everything on the ground that the hail did not destroy. Pharaoh had admitted his sin again and even compromised in offering to let only the men go. However, God cared for all His people – women and children included – and his compromise was not good enough.

9. Darkness [10:21-29]

Pharaoh promised to release God's people one last time, but his heart was hardened and he broke his promise. God sent darkness to the land in contrast to the many Egyptian sun gods: Re, Ammon-re, Aten, Atum, Horus, and Thoth (moon god). By the end of the ninth plague, Pharaoh threatened Moses' life and sent him away.

DRAWING OUT **DEEPER MEANINGS**

Are There Contradictions?

If you are reading the plagues in order, you might notice in Exodus 9:6 all the Egyptian livestock had died, yet in Exodus 9:19 livestock that were left outside were in danger of being killed by the hail. One can reasonably ask, "From where did the cows come? Weren't they all dead?" This can be explained by realizing that days, weeks, or months could have separated the plagues. By having a few days or weeks before the hailstorm, the Egyptians could have bought more livestock from traders passing through or took some of the livestock God spared from the Israelites.

Pharaoh's Compromises

When reading the last few plagues, we notice that Pharaoh acted differently versus the previous plagues. Pharaoh finally listened to his servants [10:7] and brought back Moses and Aaron to his presence. Pharaoh started to admit his sins, but one can infer that his confessions were not all that serious [9:27]. In particular, notice how Pharaoh started to give in (partially) to the demands: he let the people go worship within the land [8:25], he let them go worship without their "little ones" [10:9-11], and he let them go worship without their flocks and herds [10:24]. Pharaoh was not fooling Moses or the Lord; he only tried to compromise in a way that he could maintain some control over the Israelites. Pharaoh continued to ignore the Lord and maintained a stubborn and hard heart.

DRAWING OUT **TAKE AWAYS**

Three things you should remember after reviewing this lesson:

1. Repentance is More Than Just Being Sorry

Did you notice Pharaoh's sorrow? In the plagues of hail and locusts he admitted to having sinned! Yet did Pharaoh repent? The concept of repentance is more than just recognizing your sin and being sorry for it; it is letting that sorrow lead to a change of action. In other words, true repentance is a change of heart that leads to a change of conduct. May we not be like Pharaoh, but rather let our hearts be changed and let that lead to a change of action in our lives when we recognize our sin.

2. Evidence, Understanding, and Controversy

There should be no doubt that God brought these plagues to Egypt with His own finger [8:19]. Yet, critics of the Bible will insist that contradictions exist with these plagues. There are things about God and the plagues that we just cannot explain, but that does not mean God isn't real and did not bring about the plagues. If we are expected to have answers to every single small detail of God (including His divine actions and abilities), then we should give up now. God showed Egypt His power, Moses His power, the Israelites His power, and God has shown us His power. There is overwhelming evidence that God is behind these signs and wonders. We need to examine the evidence for God and have faith in Him when we are challenged in our belief. At the same time, however, we need to realize we don't have the capacity (or God's expectation) to understand every intricate detail of Him and/or His actions, even when they might sound contradictory, illogical, or miraculous.

3. Complete Surrender

Human beings have a problem with completely giving their all. Notice what Pharaoh did: he let God's people leave, but he would not let their livestock go with them. Pharaoh had a hard time completely giving in to God's demands. Instead of completely giving his all to God, Pharaoh "killed the messenger" and placed blame on someone other than himself. When we are told by God to change our behavior, we should not act like Pharaoh and only give part of our lives or make compromises. True subjection and service to God does not come with half-hearted compromises, but humble submittance to His whole will. Let us remove our pride and give our whole lives and heart to God and His word.

DRAWING OUT **THOUGHT QUESTIONS**

1. Were the plagues miracles from God? Compare the purpose of the plagues with the purpose of Christ's miracles in the New Testament. __

_____

_____

_____

_____

2. How was the Nile River used previously in the narrative and what might
   be ironic about it being turned into blood? _____

   _____

   _____

   _____

3. Why do the first three plagues affect the lands of Egypt and Goshen,
   while the other plagues only affect Egypt? _____

   _____

   _____

   _____

4. How does Romans 1:24ff help explain Pharaoh's hard heart? _____

   _____

   _____

   _____

5. According to Exodus 9:15f, why did God not simply wipe out the
   Egyptians (thus freeing His people)? _____

   _____

   _____

   _____

FREE AT LAST: THE PASSOVER

Exodus 11-13:16

DRAWING OUT **HIGHLIGHTS**

- Moses is warned that the death of all the firstborns will plague Egypt
- Moses gives instructions regarding the Passover and the Feast of Unleavened Bread
- The angel of the Lord kills all the firstborns in Egypt during the middle of the night
- After four hundred thirty years of slavery, Pharaoh finally agrees to let the people go
- The Feast of Unleavened Bread and the Israelites' firstborns are to be memorials of this milestone event

DRAWING OUT **CONTEXT**

After nine plagues against Egypt, God was ready to give the one and final message to Pharaoh that proclaims He is the only all-powerful God. God told Moses that the angel of the Lord would pass through Egypt in the middle of the night and kill any and every firstborn other than those of the Israelites. While nothing would be a threat to or would affect the Israelite people, every Egyptian household would be affected [11:1-10].

After God told Moses of what was to come, He then gave instructions for the people in preparation for the Passover. A spotless lamb was to be prepared, its blood sprinkled on the doorposts, and a meal eaten consisting of the lamb along with bitter herbs and unleavened bread. They were to eat this meal dressed and ready to go, complete with their sandals on and staffs in-hand [12:1-11]. The blood on the doorposts would be a sign to God and He would 'pass over' those houses during the night, not killing any of the firstborns.

God then gave instructions for the Feast of Unleavened Bread, a seven day memorial feast that the Israelites were to keep in honor of God bringing them out of bondage [12:14-20]. Moses relayed this information to the people and prepared them for what was to come. At midnight, the angel of the Lord came and killed all the firstborns in Egypt which caused Pharaoh to summon Moses and Aaron and release the Israelites. After over four hundred years in slavery, over six hundred thousand Israelites began to leave the land of Egypt, just as the Lord had promised would happen [12:29-51]. God commanded that the firstborn of the Israelites be consecrated and kept as a memorial (in addition to the feast) so the people and their future generations might remember how God redeemed His people, bringing them out of Egypt [13:1-16].

DRAWING OUT **DEEPER MEANINGS**

Why Kill All the Firstborns?

The text tells us that not one Egyptian household would be unaffected by the tenth plague. Some may beg the question in their minds, "Was this really fair to all the Egyptians? Did God go too far? After all, it was Pharaoh that did not listen to Moses/God and not the Egyptian people..." The overwhelming response to this line of thinking must be this: God is a righteous judge. We don't know all the circumstances surrounding the Egyptians themselves, but do know God acts in the way that He deems appropriate and necessary. Who are we to question that? When considering the Egyptians, we know that they treated the Israelites like property and made their lives bitter (cf. Ex 1:13f). They were not without blame. Furthermore, begging questions of God's judgement and actions against the Egyptian people can take our focus off the victims (the Israelites) much like what happens when we attempt to make excuses or attempt to shift the blame off of someone who is guilty of a crime and question their punishment; we make it more about the guilty party instead of the victim. We must not question the Judge. We must always trust in God's decisions and know that He is always just (cf. Job 34:12).

A Lasting Memorial for the People

Holidays are days throughout the year when we remember certain events. For the Israelites, God just didn't set aside a time of the year or a single day for this memorial, He arranged their calendar around it [12:2]. For seven days the Israelites were to eat unleavened bread, culminating in a feast on the seventh day. The Lord said they were to tell their children that this feast was a memorial for what He did when He brought the people out of Egypt. Not only did the Lord bring the people out of bondage, but He was going to bring them into a promised land. The Lord gave further instructions regarding the memorial that included what to tell their children when they ask, "What does this [feast] mean?" Their response was to include the fact that their firstborns now belong to the Lord for what He did in bringing them out of Egypt. Exodus 13:9 makes it clear that they were to be exposed to the memorial (and/or the event it stood for) nearly all the time, as if it was a physical mark upon their bodies. They were always to be talking, teaching, or commemorating this event. It's a never-ending holiday of sorts that is still practiced by Jews to this very day. To the Christian, our "never-ending holiday" is the memorial of Jesus' death that brought us out of bondage and will lead us into our promised land.

DRAWING OUT **TAKE AWAYS**

Three things you should remember after reviewing this lesson:

1. God Means What He Says

When God says He will do something, we better believe and know He will. God does not operate in human time or timetables (cf. 2 Pet 3:8), so while it might be a matter of "when" to us, we can be assured that the "when" is completely in God's hands and control; we might not even live to see the "when." Was over four hundred years too long to be in Egyptian slavery? Was over fourteen hundred more years too long to introduce a Savior into the world? Has over two thousand more years been too long for His return? We should not be questioning God's timing, but instead be reassured that all of His promises have and will come true. The Israelites were set free, Jesus came and died for the salvation of all men, and He will return at the final judgement. Preparing ourselves and telling others about what God has done and will do are more important than trying to determine when. Moses gave Pharaoh a warning of what was to come, which he did not heed. We too are given a warning (cf. Rom 14:10-12; Matt 25:31ff; Rev 20:11-15); are we going to heed the warning before it's too late?

2. The "Firstborns" Belong to God

To the Egyptians, the firstborn was said to belong to the gods. In contrast, God was now claiming the Israelites' firstborns for Himself. Even Jesus – the firstborn of Mary – was dedicated to God just as instructed under the old law (Luke 2:22-24). God also claimed the first and unblemished livestock and if the Israelites did not sacrifice their first and best, they were condemned for it. Malachi 1:8 even tells us such a sacrifice was "evil." Still today, God wants our "firstborns" – our first and our very best of everything, even ourselves. Romans 12:1 tells us that we are to be a holy, living sacrifice ("holy" meaning set apart for a purpose, just as the firstborns of old were set apart for God). Since God saves the Christian from bondage as He did the Israelites, the Christian is to give Him his or her best of everything – their "firstborns."

3. The Lord's Supper Parallels the Passover Memorial

The Lord's Supper is a memorial Christians take part in each week, just as the Israelites took part in the Passover memorial each year. The parallels are many:

• The Israelites were delivered from bondage in Egypt; Christians are delivered from the bondage of sin.
• The blood on the doorposts saved the Israelites from death; the shed blood of Jesus saves Christians from death.
• Both involve elements of unleavened bread and 'blood.'
• Both proclaim a message: "God delivered us from the Egyptians" to the Israelites [12:26f] and "God delivered us from sin" to the Christians (1 Cor 11:26).

Some of these connections are made specifically in the New Testament. For example, in 1 Corinthians 5:7, Paul refers to Jesus as the antitype to the Passover lamb and in 1 Peter 1:19, Jesus – the lamb of God – is described as being without spot or blemish, just as the Passover lamb was to be.

DRAWING OUT **THOUGHT QUESTIONS**

1. Why would killing the firstborn of Pharaoh be a significant blow as the current ruler of Egypt? _____

_____

_____

_____

2. How does the relationship between Moses and the Egyptians in Exodus 11:3 and 12:36 differ from that of Moses and Pharaoh? Are there any applications that can be drawn from their differences? _____

_____

_____

_____

_____

3. What is the meaning and significance of "...not even a dog will bark" against the Israelites in Exodus 11:7? _____

_____

_____

_____

_____

4. Why does Pharaoh say "...but bless me also" in Exodus 12:32? What does this mean or imply? _____

_____

_____

_____

5. In addition to the four already stated, what other connections can be drawn between the Passover/Feast of Unleavened Bread and the death of Jesus/the Lord's Supper? _____

_____

_____

_____

Map of the Exodus

The traditional path of the Israelites and location of Mount Sinai (Mount Horeb).

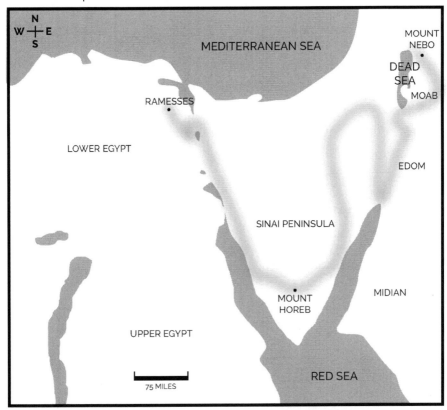

LESSON SIX
PARTING WAYS AND WATER
Exodus 13:17-15:21

DRAWING OUT **HIGHLIGHTS**

- The Israelites begin to leave Egypt by way of the desert and the Red Sea
- Moses takes Joseph's bones with them
- The Lord leads them in a pillar of cloud by day and a pillar of fire by night
- Pharaoh regrets letting the Israelites go and begins to chase after them
- Moses parts the Red Sea allowing the Israelites to walk between the divided water
- Moses returns the Red Sea to its normal state while the Egyptians are passing through, killing all of them
- Moses and the Israelites sing a song of praise and thanksgiving to God

DRAWING OUT **CONTEXT**

Concerned that the Israelites may change their minds and want to return to Egypt, God led the people out of Egypt via an untraditional route – the desert leading to the Red Sea. Moses took the bones of Joseph along with them, since Joseph had said they would carry his bones when they left Egypt [13:19]. Guiding them on their journey was the Lord who appeared as a pillar of cloud during the day and as a pillar of fire by night; they could travel at any time of the day or night.

The Lord told Moses to have the people camp before they reached the sea in an effort to make Pharaoh think the Israelites were confused and lost in the desert. However, this was exactly the Lord's plan as He then hardened Pharaoh's heart. Regretting letting them go and now believing they were lost and vulnerable, Pharaoh began to chase after the people [14:1-9]. When the Israelites saw the Egyptians coming, they were very afraid and began to question the Lord and Moses, asking if they were led to the desert simply to die and stating that it would have been better for them to have stayed in Egypt. Moses told the people not to be afraid and stated that the Lord will provide and will "fight for you" [14:10-14].

As they approached the Red Sea, the Lord told Moses to lift his staff which then divided the sea in half, creating a dry walkway for the Israelites. The cloud then moved between the Israelites and the Egyptians so they could not catch up with the Israelites while they passed through the sea during the night. In the morning when the Egyptians attempted to pass through the sea and chase after the Israelites, Moses lifted his staff again and the waters returned to their normal state, crashing down upon and killing all of the Egyptians [14:16-30].

When the Israelites saw what had happened and how the Lord delivered them, they feared and believed in the Lord. Moses and the people then sang a song to the Lord that is recorded for us in chapter fifteen. The song of triumph offers praise and thanksgiving to the Lord while recounting the events that had just taken place [14:31-15:21].

DRAWING OUT **DEEPER MEANINGS**

A Little Too Late to Do the Right Thing Now

As we saw with the plagues and Pharaoh's refusal to let the Israelites go, God continued to harden Pharaoh's heart. Here it's seen in the fact that Pharaoh pursued the Israelites and chased after them, after he'd already released them [14:3f]. Pharaoh was more than acquainted at this point with the Lord, His powers, and His abilities. So in changing his mind and attempting to capture the Israelites, he was deliberately going against the all-powerful God. He had gone against God so many times already that enough was enough, and God judged him by the hardening of his heart for a last time. A parallel is seen in Romans 1:21-28 where God also judges those who are familiar with Him and yet continue to go against

Him. While we have free will, if we continually reject God, there may come a time when it's too late to change and God will judge us or "give us up" (Rom 1:28) to our own desires. This is exactly what happened with Pharaoh.

God's Divine Intervention at the Red Sea

Where exactly was the portion of the Red Sea where the Israelites passed? No one knows. In fact, the Red Sea could have included other nearby bodies or sections of water that are not referred to as part of the Red Sea today. No matter what or where this body of water was, it's important to note that it was not a shallow swamp where the Israelites passed; the opposite, in fact. The only way the Israelites could have gotten through the sea was with God's help, otherwise it would have been impossible because of its vast size/depth of the water. This is further confirmed by the fact that the Egyptians all drowned and died when the water returned to its normal state, which would not happen naturally to an army of people in shallow, swampy water. While some may try to determine its exact location today or attempt to explain how this event happened, it's important that we understand this was a miracle from God. God alone saved His people by His intervention and control of the water (cf. Psalm 66:6; 78:13; 106:9; 136:13).

DRAWING OUT **TAKE AWAYS**

Three things you should remember after reviewing this lesson:

1. When Fear Takes Over

The second the Israelites saw the Egyptians coming for them after their release they became afraid. They blamed Moses, questioned him and the Lord, and panicked. But why? Did they forget all the things the Lord had just accomplished? And that He was with them as the pillar of cloud/fire? In the New Testament, Jesus' disciples were in a boat with Jesus himself and as soon as a violent storm came, they too became afraid (Matt 8:23-27). Why do God's people become afraid – or worse, forsake and question God – when they know what God has done and what He's capable of doing? David wrote in Psalm 56:3f that when he is afraid, he will trust in God and will not fear man. David experienced fear, but chose to trust in God. We can do the same. When we become afraid, think of all God has done (even in the account of the Red Sea) and how there is nothing God cannot handle or remove from us if it is in His will to do so. Moses said it best when he responded to the people after they expressed their fear: "Stand still and see the salvation of the Lord" [14:13]. Moses knew the enemy was near, but he knew God was also near and that trumped his fear.

2. Going From Nowhere to Somewhere

Although the Israelites could have left Egypt and taken a more direct route to eventually reach the promised land, they did not. The Lord took them in a direction that was indirect and probably appeared to be a "road to nowhere." But while the people may have thought they were going nowhere, God was taking them somewhere. He took them in a direction where: His power would be displayed (by the crossing at the Red Sea), they would not become afraid, turn around and go back, and where they would learn to rely on Him. He would provide for them in difficult circumstances (e.g., in the middle of the wilderness). Sometimes we too may think we are on a "road to nowhere" in our lives – we might become fearful, lose faith, or question God. However, we need to remember that God is faithful even in hard times, sad times, and when we feel like our lives are going nowhere. We need to remember that we might experience circumstances that will teach us to better rely on and trust in God, circumstances that may test our faith, and circumstances that will help us grow. The Israelites didn't get to take the direct route and we might not either. But we're not going "nowhere" if we always trust in God, He's taking us "somewhere" just like He did the Israelites – a promised land (cf. Matt 6:25-34).

3. Salvation Through Water

The parting of the Red Sea is one of, if not the most, popular accounts in the Old Testament to modern readers. While it may be popular due to its grand, demonstrative showing of God's power or the fact that it is the final event that solidified the Israelites' freedom, the event is of major importance. But the event also has importance in its symbolic nature, just as other Old Testament accounts do. The Israelites were saved from destruction through the use of water. The Israelites entered into the promised land by the use of water at the Jordan River. Noah and his family were saved from destruction by water. Today, Christians are saved through the use of water baptism. From scripture we can clearly see a pattern when it comes to the use of water. Paul uses the expression in 1 Corinthians 10:1 that the people were "baptized into Moses in the cloud and in the sea" and Peter makes the argument in 1 Peter 3:20f that Christian baptism corresponds to Noah's ark. The Red Sea event is an excellent parallel to the Christian being saved by water baptism; we might desire to leave a life of bondage (i.e., sin), but it's not until we "pass through the sea" that we are truly saved, entering into a new life led by God, bound for a promised land. It was only after the Israelites passed through the Red Sea that they were saved and it's only after we're baptized that we can be saved (cf. Acts 2:38; 1 Pet 3:21; Acts 22:16; Gal 3:27).

DRAWING OUT **THOUGHT QUESTIONS**

1. After all they had gone through to be set free, why would the Israelites have changed their minds, wanting to return to their lives of slavery in Egypt? _____

_____

_____

_____

2. Where else do we see the Lord appearing in or by fire and smoke/ clouds within scripture? _____

_____

_____

_____

3. The Jews/Israelites are also referred to as the "Hebrews" – what is the origin and meaning of this term? _____

_____

_____

_____

4. What finally caused the Egyptians to recognize God's active involvement in the events at the Red Sea? _____

_____

_____

_____

5. Compare and note any similarities between the song of Moses in Exodus 15 with the song of Moses quoted in Revelation 15. ___

_____

_____

_____

_____

LESSON SEVEN
COMPLAINING WITH NO REFRAINING
Exodus 15:22-18:27

DRAWING OUT **HIGHLIGHTS**

- The Israelites travel through the wilderness of Shur, where Moses throws a log into the water to make it sweet
- The Israelites travel through the wilderness of Sin, where God provides manna and quail for the people during their wandering
- While in the wilderness of Sin, the Israelites camp at Rephidim, defeat Amalek, and meet with Jethro to appoint judges over the people

DRAWING OUT **CONTEXT**

After having delivered His people through the Red Sea, God led the Israelites on a three-day journey through the wilderness of Shur. During this time in Shur the Israelites camped at Marah [15:23]. It is there that God's people grumbled about the water being bitter, in which God responded by telling Moses to throw a log into the water to turn it sweet [15:25]. Still in the wilderness of Shur, Moses led the people through Elim, a place with twelve wells and seventy palm trees to shade the Israelites [15:27].

After the wilderness of Shur, the Israelites journeyed through the wilderness of Sin. While in the wilderness and about one month removed from Egyptian captivity, God's people complained again about their food situation [16:2]. In response, the Lord provided quail and manna for the people [16:4f], with the condition to store up extra on the sixth day of the week to prepare them for a seventh "day of rest." This manna was gathered by Moses in a pot that would eventually be placed in the Ark of the Covenant [16:33].

The journey through the wilderness of Sin took place in many stages, one of which consisted of a camping at Rephidim [17:1f]. While at Rephidim, the Israelites experienced many unique events, but not before complaining again about the lack of water. Moses did as God commanded and struck a rock to produce fresh water for the people to drink [17:6]. While in Rephidim, the Amalekites attacked the Israelite stragglers. With Joshua leading the battle, Moses held his arms up in the air (with the help of Aaron and Hur), which led to a resounding victory for God's people [17:8f].

While still in Rephidim, Moses' father-in-law (Jethro) brought Zipporah (Moses' wife) and Gershom and Eliezer (Moses' sons) to Moses [18:2f]. Jethro joined Moses in a period of worship to God, then gave Moses some advice concerning the appointment of judges [18:13f]. The judges Moses appointed helped relieve pressure from doing the job himself and provided a systematic approach to administering justice. This whole section of wandering in the wilderness of Shur and Sin took place within the span of forty to forty-five days after Egyptian bondage.

DRAWING OUT **DEEPER MEANINGS**

Master of Water, Power of Wood

While in Shur the people complained about the water being bitter. God demonstrated His power by turning the bitter water into sweet water. God is the master of this world, including water. This calls back to the first plague where God showed mastery over the Nile River by turning its water into blood (Ex 7:14-25). Christ also showed mastery over water by turning water into wine (John 2:1-11). Notice the medium of this water transformation: a log. The imagery of a life-saving tree is seen throughout the Bible, specifically in the cross of Christ. We need to drink the life-saving water that is made sweet by Calvary's tree.

Drink From the Spiritual Rock

In Exodus 17 we see God provided for His people by producing water out of a rock at Rephidim. Moses was instructed to strike the rock, providing water for a thirsty people. The rock was there for the people, providing substance in their greatest need. In comparison, Christ is our rock that was stricken for us during our time of greatest need. We read of this spiritual rock in 1 Corinthians 10:4...how Christ was struck with a rod of suffering and living water flowed out for us. Just as God provided for His people in the Old Testament, God provides for His people in the New Testament with living water to drink.

DRAWING OUT **TAKE AWAYS**

Three things you should remember after reviewing this lesson:

1. Be Grateful and Do Not Complain

It is incredible to see how quickly the Israelites started to complain and lose faith in God. Not even one week since leaving Egypt and they already started to complain. We can empathize with them a little, understanding how precious water is to life and how their expectations after deliverance were not exactly met. But there was no excuse to complain to the same God that just released them from hundreds of years of slavery! Why did the people complain? Psalm 106:12f tells us the reason: the people forgot. We often read the phrase "we are a forgetful people," and while that may be true, what are we really forgetting? When we don't look back and remember past deliverances from oppression/sin, we can forget and not be grateful. God's people did not remember that the Lord delivered them from slavery, and we cannot forget that He has delivered us from the bondage of sin. A grateful heart is a heart that remembers past deliverances and learns not to grumble while living in a twisted and crooked society (cf. Phil 2:5-18).

2. Free Gifts From God Require Obedience

God made provisions to help His people. He gave them manna and quail to sustain them throughout their journey, but He did not give those to them without conditions. They had to go out and collect the food with their hands. They had to collect extra on the sixth day. They could not keep extra overnight on the other days. God gives us the perfect free gift of salvation, but just because it is "free" does not mean we don't have to do anything. We need to obey God to receive the blessings He offers us.

When we are blessed by God, we are commanded to share those blessings with others. The similar language of Exodus 16 is used in 2 Corinthians 8:13 where we learn gifts of physical blessings should be used to help support other brethren. God does not give so that we can keep receiving and hoard up riches.

3. We Have an Amazing Story to Tell

Notice the topics Moses and Jethro discussed in Exodus 18. They first asked how each other were doing [18:7], much like we would today when we see friends we haven't seen in years. Then Moses told Jethro three things: the miracles of God with the Egyptians, the hardships of travel, and God's deliverance. Jethro's response was one of praise and worship to God for all that He had done for Moses and the people. Moses gave God the credit and pointed to Him in front of his family. It is very encouraging to see family members talk about how great the Lord is, but of course, Moses told Jethro these things because what God did was incredible! We, like Moses, have an incredible story to tell – one that is much more amazing than that of the exodus. God has delivered His people from the bondage of sin! We need to be excited to tell our physical families, spiritual families, and friends about the amazing story of God delivering us from sin and the life we can now live in Christ.

DRAWING OUT **THOUGHT QUESTIONS**

1. Using the Israelites as a negative example, how can we learn to trust in the Lord during times of adversity? _____

_____

_____

_____

2. Why did the Israelites complain to God so quickly after leaving Egypt?

_____

_____

_____

3. What does it mean in Exodus 17:2, 7 when it says the Israelites "tested" or "tempted" the Lord? _____

_____

_____

_____

4. What eventually happened to the nation of Amalek? Hint: Exodus 17:14; 1 Samuel 15. _____

_____

_____

_____

5. How can we get excited to tell our friends and families about Jesus? _____

_____

_____

_____

LESSON EIGHT
THE TEN COMMANDMENTS

Exodus 19-20:21

DRAWING OUT **HIGHLIGHTS**

- The Israelites reach the desert of Sinai
- The people agree to obey God's commands so they can be His chosen people
- God announces that He will make an appearance on Mount Sinai and the people must prepare themselves
- The presence of God is seen on the mountain in a violent storm with fire, smoke, thunder, and wind
- Moses goes up on the mountain and relays all that the Lord told him to the people, including the Ten Commandments
- The people tremble in fear when they see the mountain and at the thought of God speaking to them directly

DRAWING OUT **CONTEXT**

The Israelites arrived and camped in the desert of Sinai, next to the mountain. The Lord called Moses from Mount Sinai and told him to tell the people that if they continued to follow all of His commands they would be His special people and a holy nation. Moses gathered the elders together and relayed the information; the people agreed to do all that the Lord commanded. While Moses relayed this back to the Lord, the Lord told Moses that He would speak to him in a dense cloud so the people would know God was with him. The Lord also told Moses that the people needed to be sanctified and they were not to touch or approach the mountain because in three days He was going to make an appearance to all the people [19:1-15].

With a dense cloud, thunder, and lightning at the top of the mountain, the people trembled at the bottom in the presence of God. God called Moses to come up the mountain and told him to relay His words to the people [19:16-25]. His words included the following, known as the Ten Commandments:

1. You shall have no other gods before Me [20:2f]
   If the people wish to be God's chosen people and a holy nation, they can only recognize Him as their God. As with other covenants, this agreement is between two parties. In this case, it's the Israelites and God; no other parties, gods, etc. are to be involved and nothing is to come before God.

2. You shall not make nor worship a carved image [20:4-6]
   The people were never to attempt to make God into an earthly image/ something that is physical. God is not physical and does not dwell in the physical, but rather the spiritual. When people attempt to form or fashion their god into a human-based image or object, they are in control over what they want their god to look like or to "be." God is above any and everything that can be created in this world and nothing created should be worshiped to represent Him.

3. You shall not take the name of the Lord in vain [20:7]
   We know that our name is important, our reputation is important, and we are even cautious to invoke others' names depending on the circumstances. We understand that using (or invoking) a person's name is almost as if we're invoking themselves – the essence of the actual person. This is the same with God. His name goes to who He is. If His name is used in an empty, vain, or careless way, it is as if we are treating Him in the same way. God is holy and set apart; His name is hallowed and should be used in ways that only characterize God as such. The people were never to disgrace God's name.

4. Remember the Sabbath day to set it apart as holy [20:8-11]
   This commandment was specific to the old law and reminiscent of God creating for six days and resting on the seventh during the time of creation (Gen 2:3). The people were to rest and not work on the Sabbath day as a possible time to reflect on the providing and giving nature of God, not being distracted by their other day-to-day affairs.

5. Honor your father and your mother [20:12]

The Israelites relied on God and could do nothing alone. We are similar in that there are times when we need the reliance and help of others, including our parents. Honoring one's father and mother shows we recognize that we cannot do it all on our own; someone else took the time and effort to care for us. Furthermore, if one cannot submit to and respect his or her own parents, how can he or she submit to God?

6. You shall not murder [20:13]

All God-given life is important and the people have no right to take that away from anyone. Murder can be viewed as the ultimate form of pride, revenge, and covetousness.

7. You shall not commit adultery [20:14]

Similar to this covenant, the marriage covenant is between two parties and no one in the covenant is allowed to break the agreement; allowing any outsiders to be involved. No one is to be involved or affect a marriage covenant by interfering with the sanctity of the marriage and the marital, sexual relationship. The people are to respect marriage and control their desires.

8. You shall not steal [20:15]

The people were to be content with what they had. Their reliance should be on God and not in the accumulation of objects...let alone items God has blessed others to possess. The people were not to obtain what was not rightfully theirs.

9. You shall not give false testimony [20:16]

Honesty and truthfulness are fundamental in covenant agreements, in our character, and even in the taking of personal responsibility. God is truth. His word is truth. The people were not to avoid telling the truth because it might cause them harm, because it's not in their best interest, the interests of others, etc. Following this commandment demonstrates one's character and integrity.

10. You shall not covet [20:17]

While the latter commandments spell out the love the people were to have for their fellow neighbors, this commandment sums them up: do not be envious. The cause for murders, adultery, stealing, and lying all come from a source of "want." The people were to be happy for their neighbors, rejoice in their good times and situations, and not give into the temptation of being envious, jealous, and contentious toward them.

After the commandments were delivered, the people became fearful when they continued to look upon the mountain covered with dark clouds, storms, and smoke. They told Moses that they would listen to God, but they did not want God to speak to them, lest they die. Moses explained that God was testing them – causing the fear – so they would not sin [20:18-21].

DRAWING OUT **DEEPER MEANINGS**

Mount Sinai Itself

While the exact mountain the Bible refers to as Mount Sinai is unknown, a traditional site is Mount Horeb (also known as Jebel Musa) in the Sinai Peninsula. This mountain is over 7,400 feet at its highest point. Today there stands a mosque, chapel, and "Moses' cave" (where he was said to have waited after ascending to receive the commandments) at the top of the mountain. While there is debate over the exact mountain and its location, it is still fascinating to realize that on one of those mountains in that portion of the world, God, Moses, and the Israelite people all met for the giving of the law. See the map that appears on page 36.

Classifying the Ten Commandments

The Ten Commandments can be separated into two groups: those relating to God and those relating to fellow men. As the Mosaic Law unfolds in later chapters, we see more specific laws with additional groupings and specific purposes, but the Ten Commandments reveal the essence of the law in these two groups.

In the four commandments relating to God, it's important to note that the people entered an agreement with: a God who has acted in history (a proven track record), a God who is spiritual/invisible and not be represented by an idol or image, a God whose name must be taken seriously and not discounted, and a God who prohibited work on the seventh day – a divine order.

In the six commandments that relate to fellow men, the people were to: respect their parents (rebellious children could be stoned!), not murder one another, only have sex within the marriage relationship, not steal from one another, be truthful and honest, and not wrongfully desire things that were not theirs.

More on Covenants

A covenant (also called an agreement, treaty, contract, etc.) normally has several elements including responsibilities, benefits, and penalties. The Mosaic Law is no exception. Upon further inspection of the Law, we can see that it closely follows that of a "Suzerainty Treaty" used by the Hittites. This kind of document would explain the relationship between a ruler and his subjects. In addition to the elements found in basic covenants, this format contains several additional elements that structure the Mosaic Law:

• Preamble (the author; Ex 20:2)
• Prologue (what the ruler has done; Ex 19:4)
• Stipulations (rules of the agreement/the commandments; Ex 20:2-17)
• Blessings and cursings (consequences in keeping/forsaking the agreement; Ex 23:20-22)
• Acceptance (the subjects' agreement; Ex 24:3)

It is very likely that Moses (who grew up in Egypt) would have been familiar with this type of agreement used by the Hittites. This understanding could have demonstrated to the people more about the nature of the agreement, rather than just its contents.

DRAWING OUT **TAKE AWAYS**

Three things you should remember after reviewing this lesson:

1. Christians Are Now God's Chosen People

Imagine if God told you that He chose you to be a part of His special people, His holy nation. What excitement, joy, and humility one would feel! That's exactly what happened to the people at the foot of Mount Sinai – God chose them to be His people. They simply had to follow His commands and obey Him, and God would claim them as His own. This is the same today with Christians. God – through Jesus – has chosen Christians as another group of people to be His special people and holy nation (Eph 1:4). If one will obey and put his or her faith in God's Son, God will claim him or her as His own (1 Pet 2:9). Yet, it's an offer that many refuse, give up on, or neglect. In the initial promises to Abraham, God stated that all nations would be blessed (Gen 12:1-3). Through Moses and the Israelites, a specific group of people was blessed. But now through Jesus, anyone (i.e., all nations) can be blessed who simply believes in Him and obeys His commands.

2. Jesus Fulfills the Ten Commandments

In His sermon on the mount in Matthew 5:17-48, Jesus makes reference to the Ten Commandments and says that He did not come to destroy the Mosaic Law, but instead to fulfill it. What does that mean? Many view the Old Law as specific commands and ordinances regarding one's behavior. Jesus, however, makes it clear that the Old Law was always about more than just behavior; it was about one's heart and motivations. Time and time again he quotes an example commandment (e.g., "you shall not murder" – Matt 5:21) and then demonstrates the heart of the commandment (e.g., "everyone who is angry..." – Matt 5:22). Jesus' continual statement of "but I say to you" is not to be taken as Him changing the commandment, but revealing what the deeper meaning and application is. While some argue that the Old Testament is all about physical laws and the New Testament is all about the heart, it's clear from His sermon that Jesus is telling the people God has been concerned with their hearts all along.

3. The Ten Commandments in Today's World

While we're not under the Mosaic Law today, each of the Ten Commandments is repeated inside the New Testament law (except for the Sabbath Day observance). While the Ten Commandments were given in a different time and place, consider how even today they are applicable in ways you might not have considered. For example, while "thou shalt not murder" may not be something the average Christian (or non-Christian) may struggle with and might seem foreign to the modern-day Christian (i.e., "I would never do that"), in today's world there are murders that the average person and Christian may be tempted to become involved in: abortions. Also consider "thou shalt not steal" – another commandment that may seem foreign to us. But what about online/digital content such as music, movies, software, etc. or fraudulent income taxes and business dealings? Stealing doesn't have to be robbing a store and murder doesn't have to be at gun point for these commandments to still have their place in our world today.

DRAWING OUT **THOUGHT QUESTIONS**

1. How can one take God's name in vain other than using His name as a "swear word?" _____

_____

_____

_____

2. Explain the significance of keeping the Sabbath day as a commandment. Do Christians keep a "Sabbath day?" What do Seventh-day Adventists believe? _____

_____

_____

3. How does a covenant from God (i.e., the Mosaic Law) differ from a promise (e.g., made to Abraham, David, and through Jesus) from God?

_____

_____

_____

4. Explain how Jesus "fulfilled" the Ten Commandments, but did not "abolish" them. _____

_____

_____

_____

5. How does the author of Hebrews describe the scene at Mount Sinai in Hebrews 12:18-21? _____

_____

_____

_____

LESSON NINE
THE GOLDEN CALF
Exodus 32

DRAWING OUT **HIGHLIGHTS**

- Due to the delay in Moses returning from the mountain, the people ask Aaron to make them an idol since they do not know what happened to Moses
- Aaron takes gold from their jewelry, molds it into a calf, and builds an altar before it
- God is extremely angry at the people for what they have done and wants to destroy them
- Moses pleads with God and asks that His anger be subsided and the people not be destroyed
- Moses returns from the mountain and, after seeing the calf, throws down and breaks the tablets he brought back with him in anger
- Moses destroys the calf and confronts Aaron about the situation
- Over three thousand people die as a punishment and the Lord sends a plague on the people

DRAWING OUT **CONTEXT**

When the people didn't see Moses come down from the mountain, they became nervous and questioned what happened to him. Since they were not sure, they asked Aaron to make gods for them. Aaron asked for the gold from their jewelry, melted it all down and molded it into the image of a calf. The people then said that it was these gods that brought them out of Egypt. After building an altar, the people offered sacrifices and had a feast to the Lord [32:1-6].

When God saw what the people had done, He told Moses to return to them so that His anger could burn and He could destroy them for their wickedness. However, Moses tried to reason with God, reminding Him of His promises to the people and how He didn't bring them out of Egypt simply to die. God then relented over His anger [32:7-14].

Moses came down from the mountain with two tablets engraved by God. When he saw the people and what they had done, he threw the tablets on the ground, breaking them into pieces. Moses then took their golden calf, melted it down, ground it into powder, poured water on it, and forced the people to drink it [32:15-20].

Moses questioned Aaron as to how this happened and Aaron blamed it on the people claiming they "tend to evil." Moses realized then that Aaron did not have control of the people. As punishment for their sin, he ordered the people to run across the camp, killing a brother, friend, and neighbor. Over three thousand people died. Moses then returned to the mountain and asked God for His blessing on the people. God said that whoever sins against Him would not have his name written in His book and that He would indeed punish them for their sin. God then sent a plague on the people for the calf that Aaron made [32:21-35].

DRAWING OUT **DEEPER MEANINGS**

How Could Aaron Do This?

How could Aaron, the brother of Moses and witness to all that God had done, give in to the people's demand that an idol be made? While the text does not tell us, it is interesting to propose possible explanations that may help us understand how and why those we consider to be "pillars of faith" (even today) sometimes crumble. Consider these questions in regard to Aaron's actions:

• Did Aaron simply give in to a demanding crowd/peer pressure? (We're told that he had lost control of the people in Exodus 32:25.)

• Were he and the people simply influenced by the idol-worshippers around them and in their previous Egyptian history? (Since Moses did

not reappear initially, the people didn't know what happened to him
and/or possibly to their God in Exodus 32:1.)

• Did Aaron purposely give in to the people and make the idol so they
could see how ridiculous it was? Could he have agreed with them to
buy more time for Moses' return, distracting the people from their
questioning? (Both of these would imply his motives were initially good,
but turned bad.)

No matter what the cause, we know that God was angry with Aaron and
the people. Aaron blamed his actions on the people and foolishly on a
"magic fire" that could miraculously create calf-shaped objects [32:21-24].

Why a Golden Calf?

The Israelites' creation and worship of the golden calf were wrong on at
least two levels. First, it went against the commandment of not having any
other gods before God (Ex 20:3ff). Second, the idol changed their worship
and image of God. Did the Israelites really think their newly created
calf made out of gold delivered them from Egypt as they proclaimed?
Hopefully and seemingly not. The calf represented the true God who did.
In fact, they later had a feast to "the Lord," not to "the calf." But with
the influence of idol-worshippers around them, they could not resist the
need to fashion an object to represent the Lord. The people added pagan
elements to their worship of God. As if it were not enough to reject God's
commandments, what a "slap in the face" to God to be trivialized and
represented by a calf/animal that was probably based on the gods the
people knew from their time in Egypt.

How Did Moses Change God's Mind?

When God told Moses what He had witnessed and how He planned to
consume the people, Moses pleaded with God in an effort to change
His mind [32:9-14]. But note how Moses appealed to God. It was not
necessarily on behalf of the people, on himself, or on anything other than
one thing – God's glory. Moses reminded God that He was the one who
initially freed and saved the people. Being the God of Abraham, Isaac,
and Jacob (having made promises to them about their offspring), but

then consuming the people would cause them to ask, "With evil intent did [God] bring them out, to kill [the people] in the mountains and to consume them from the face of the earth?" Each appeal Moses made went to magnify God's name and reputation among the nations, to show His power and His faithfulness in His promises. Today, we too can keep the same principle in mind – when we appeal to God for anything, His glory and His magnification should be our priority.

DRAWING OUT **TAKE AWAYS**

Three things you should remember after reviewing this lesson:

1. We Must Worship in Spirit and in Truth

After the people created their golden calf, an altar was built and sacrifices, offerings, and a feast were given to the Lord. The people were still worshiping the Lord, but not in the way He wanted. In the creation of the idol itself, two commandments were already broken. Now they were using the idol in their worship. We need to always keep in mind that we worship a God who has provided us with instructions on how to worship Him, with the proper mindset and proper procedures. We cannot borrow or add to our worship elements that might seem appealing from other religions, practices, etc. nor can we take away those God-given ones we find less appealing. Jesus says we are to worship "in spirit and truth" in John 4:24...something the Israelites failed to do in their worship to God with the golden calf.

2. Sin Should Make Us Angry

When God saw what the people had done, we're told He was angry and was filled with wrath. When Moses saw what the people had done, he broke the tablets engraved on by God. In the New Testament, when Jesus saw what the people were doing in the temple (exchanging money and using it as a marketplace), He too became angry (John 2). God gets angry at sin and so should we. If we are to be holy and set apart, we are to have no association with sin. It should invoke a feeling of displeasure when we witness it, or worse, take part in it. Sometimes human anger goes too far...unjust punishments, harsh words, rejection, regretful decisions (cf. "be angry and do not sin" – Eph 4:26). But God's anger is always just – under control and always directed against sin. Sin should cause us to respond like God does, with controlled anger and wrath toward sin. When we view sin in this light, our desire to take part in it lessens and our stand for righteousness influences others. We should be thankful that we have a loving and forgiving God who, even though He has every right to be angry and punish all of us, offers us a chance at forgiveness and a chance for His wrath to be removed from our sinful actions (cf. Psalm 85:2f).

3. Jesus (Like Moses) is an Intercessor

The Israelite people had a problem. They had rejected God, sinned against Him and needed to be brought back into His good graces. Who was responsible for this? Moses. Moses was the one that pleaded with God and asked that He forgive the people. Moses was also the one who communicated in both directions: between God and the people, and the people and God. Today, Jesus plays the same role. He is our mediator – the one that communicates between Christians and God (1 Tim 2:5). Christians pray and talk to God through Jesus. Likewise, God communicates to Christians through the person of Jesus – through His words, His teachings, and His example. The book of Romans tells us that the Holy Spirit and Jesus, sitting at the right hand of God, intercede for Christians today (Rom 8:26-34). Moses was a powerful example and foreshadowing of things to come during the time of the Israelites.

DRAWING OUT **THOUGHT QUESTIONS**

1. What was the significance or rationale for creating a calf? Why a calf as opposed to any other animal or object? Where else in the Bible do we see calf idols being made and worshipped? _____

_____

_____

2. What pagan or outside religious elements might some be tempted to bring into the worship of God today? Why? _____

_____

_____

_____

3. Recount the excuses Aaron made when confronted with his creation of the golden calf. How might they parallel to excuses we might make when confronted with our sin? _____

_____

_____

_____

4. Explain the figurative use and the meaning of the phrase "stiff necked" God used to describe the people after they betrayed Him. How does the same phrase used in Acts 7:51 apply in the New Testament? _____

_____

_____

_____

5. What does Isaiah 44:16-19 say about idols and idol worship? __

_____

_____

_____

_____

LESSON TEN
THE COVENANT CONFIRMED

Exodus 24, 33-34

DRAWING OUT **HIGHLIGHTS**

- The Israelites confirm the covenant by verbal and sacrificial offerings
- God punishes the people because of their sin involving the golden calf
- Moses intercedes for the people and God shows mercy by renewing the covenant
- Moses returns from his second period of forty days on the mountain with a shiny face

DRAWING OUT **CONTEXT**

We have already seen God introduce himself to the people, initiating a Suzerainty Treaty (Ex 19). God had laid out specific stipulations in the Ten Commandments (Ex 20) with additional stipulations and blessings/cursings in the remaining chapters of Exodus and Leviticus. For now, let's focus on the last part of the Suzerainty Treaty: the acceptance from the subject.

When God first gave Moses the Ten Commandments, Moses relayed the initial law to the people [24:3]. The people verbally confirmed their commitment to follow the laws of the Lord and then offered a sacrifice to further confirm the covenant. The covenant the Lord made with His people was completely confirmed when Moses took blood from the sacrifice and threw it on the people [24:8]. It must have been a great day of joy when God and His people ratified their covenant.

But, as we already know, things changed quickly for the Israelites. The Lord called Moses back up onto the mountain [24:12-18], leaving the people alone for forty days under the leadership of Aaron and Hur. While the people were without Moses, Aaron helped them construct a golden calf (Ex 32). There were extreme consequences to the actions of the Israelites: God sent a plague (Ex 32:35), God commanded them to depart from the mountain [33:1], God sent an angel to deal with the people now instead of dealing with them Himself [33:2], and God's interactions with Moses were restricted [33:22-23].

The Israelites were shown mercy because of Moses' actions. In Exodus 33, Moses interceded for the people, asking God to show mercy on them [33:17]. Because God found favor in Moses, the Lord told Moses He would renew the covenant with the people [34:1-10]. Moses went up on Mount Sinai for a second time and stayed forty days while God relayed the law to him again [34:11-28]. During the first forty days and the second forty days on the mountain, Moses almost certainly received the full law recorded for us in Exodus, Leviticus, and Numbers. After receiving the law, Moses returned from the mountain with the skin of his face shining [34:29-35].

DRAWING OUT **DEEPER MEANINGS**

The Tent of Meeting

What was the "tent of meeting" [33:7-11]? It is clear that this could not be the Tabernacle, as the Tabernacle had not been constructed yet. The word used for "tent" in this passage is a different Hebrew word than the one used for "tabernacle." The word used for tabernacle means "a dwelling place of God," and while certainly this tent would have been a dwelling place, it was temporary. This tent did not have the same elements that the Tabernacle had, specifically an outer court that separated the people from clear eyesight of certain objects. The purpose of this tent was to provide Moses a convenient place to meet with God. It might have been a way for God to show Moses that sin changes one's relationship with God, thus the need for a new temporary tent of meeting.

Why Did Moses Wear a Veil?

When Moses first came down from the mountain where he was receiving the law for a second time, he did not realize his face was shining brightly [34:11-28]. Aaron and the people saw the bright face of Moses and vocalized their fear, but Moses eased their concerns, telling the whole congregation what God had commanded. Whenever Moses finished speaking a section, he put a veil over his face until it was time to go back and speak to the Lord. Some think this veil was used so as to not frighten the people, but that does not make sense in the context. Moses only wore the veil after speaking to the Lord and before he went to talk to the Lord. In 2 Corinthians 3:13 an explanation is given as to why Moses wore the veil: so the people would not see the shining face of Moses fade away. In other words, God did not want His people to see the glory of God fade, thus giving them encouragement to listen and keep all of His words.

DRAWING OUT **TAKE AWAYS**

Three things you should remember after reviewing this lesson:

1. "Behold the Blood of the Covenant"

When Moses read the ordinances to the people in Exodus 24, they responded with a resounding commitment to keep the commandments. Moses then took the blood that was sacrificed on the altar, threw it on the people and said, "Behold the blood of the covenant that the Lord has made with you in accordance with all these words" [24:8]. As a final act to ratify the covenant, blood was sprinkled and sacrificial meat was eaten by Moses and others. In comparison, Christ echoed the words of Moses when He instituted the Lord's Supper – "For this is My blood of the covenant, which is poured out for many for forgiveness of sins" (Matt 26:28). Like Moses eating the offering as an affirmation of the Old Covenant, we eat the Lord's Supper as an affirmation of the New Covenant we have with Jesus Christ. It is amazing that God set up a plan where every week we are reminded of the covenant we have with Christ when partaking of the emblems that symbolize His sacrifice.

2. "Please Show Me Your Glory"

God punished His people for their sin involving the golden calf. He sent a plague, He used an angel to deal with the people, and He sent them away. How serious are these consequences? Moses summed it up best when he asked, "Please show me your glory" [33:18]. Because of sin, the Lord was distancing Himself from the people; He removed His presence and glory from their midst. God was separating Himself from the people... the exact opposite of what He wanted to do! This can even be seen when God allowed Moses to only see His back while in the cleft of the rock [33:22-23]. God showed the people a direct consequence of breaking the covenant – God does not tolerate and dwell with sin. Sin has always separated us from Him (cf. Gen 2). The theme of the entire Bible is finding a way for God's glory to dwell in the midst of His people. We will see this theme develop even more when we discuss the Tabernacle.

3. "Written By the Finger of God"

The book of Exodus makes it very clear who was behind the Law. There is no doubt that the Lord was the one who initiated the covenant and penned the words of the Law. Countless times we read statements such as "I will give you" and "I have written." One of the clearest statements that shows God's complete involvement in the Law is this: "It was written with the finger of God" [31:18]. This is a simple sentence that we might skip over accidentally, but its inclusion in Exodus is no accident. Earlier in Exodus, Pharaoh's magicians exclaimed that the plague of gnats was a miracle by the finger of God (Ex 8:19). We also see Jesus claimed to work miracles by the finger of God in Luke 11:20. Today, we are often left wondering just how active a role God plays in specific circumstances in our lives. Sometimes the only conclusion we can draw is "perhaps" God caused this or that to happen. Yet, we have the assurance that God's plan for redemption is one hundred percent constructed, carried out, and overseen by the Lord Himself; in no way "perhaps." God is the one behind the Old Law, God is the one behind the New Law, and God is the mastermind of our reconciliation to Him.

DRAWING OUT **THOUGHT QUESTIONS**

1. What were the punishments for the golden calf and why were they so
   severe? _____

   _____

   _____

2. How do we know the Old Covenant was confirmed by God's people?

   _____

   _____

   _____

3. According to 2 Corinthians 3:7-18, what are some New Testament
   applications that can be made from Moses' veil? _____

   _____

   _____

   _____

4. What evidences in the text indicate that Moses was more concerned
   with Israel as a whole, rather than just himself as an individual? Hint:
   Exodus 33:14f. _____

   _____

   _____

   _____

5. Describe the attributes of God in Exodus 34:7f. Has God changed

since then? _____

_____

_____

_____

LESSON ELEVEN
FEASTS, FESTIVALS, AND SACRIFICES

Exodus 23:10-19; Leviticus 1-7, 16, 23-25

DRAWING OUT **HIGHLIGHTS**

- While on Mount Sinai for two separate forty day periods, God gives Moses various laws
- God organizes five types of offerings which are all used in different types of worship
- The Jews are to keep a variety of festivals and feasts in dedication to the Lord

DRAWING OUT **CONTEXT**

After the events in Exodus 24, Moses went up to Mount Sinai for forty days. Moses then went back up to Mount Sinai a second time for forty more days. What exactly did God communicate to Moses the first time compared to the second time? We do not know exactly which commands were given to Moses on which occasion, but we do know God gave Moses various instructions during this eighty day period.

Offerings

Parts of the instructions given were specific rules for sacrifices, feasts, and festivals the people were to observe. In Leviticus 1-7, there is a summary of the five types of sacrifices the Israelites could offer. The sacrifices listed below are general summations, with some exceptions for specific circumstances. These offerings could be made on behalf of an individual or on behalf of the entire congregation.

• Burnt Offerings (Lev 1:3-17; 6:8-13)

These sacrifices were the most common and involved the complete consumption of an animal. All parts of a male bull, sheep, goat, dove, or pigeon were consumed by fire, except for their hides [1:9; 7:8]. These clean animals were slaughtered and skinned by the offerer, then blood was sprinkled around the altar by a priest. No part of the offering was eaten and the ashes were taken by the priest and scattered outside the camp in a clean place.

• Meal/Grain Offerings (Lev 2:1-16; 6:14-23; Num 15:1-16)

Meal offerings, often times called grain or meat (KJV) offerings, were always made when any "fleshly" offering was made (i.e., a burnt offering or any other animal sacrifice). This sacrifice consisted of flour, oil, incense, salt, frankincense, and other ingredients that varied by the specific circumstance of the sacrifice. If offered by an individual other than a priest, a portion of the offering went to the priests for their consumption. If a meal offering was made on behalf of a priest, the entire offering was burned and consumed in the fire.

• Peace Offerings (Lev 3:1-17; 7:11-21; 22:29-30)

Peace offerings signified that things were right (or for a desire for things to be right) between the offerer and God. There were three main purposes for a peace offering: making a vow, an offering of thanksgiving, and a freewill offering by an individual. Although specifics vary depending on circumstances, peace offerings were eaten by both offerer and priest.

• Sin Offerings (Lev 4:1-5:13)

Sin offerings are more detailed in Leviticus than the other four offerings, and understandably so. The regulations for sin offerings differed depending on the type of sin and who committed it. Priests were required to bring a bull, kings and rulers were required to bring an unblemished male goat, and the common people were required to bring a female goat or lamb. For the most part, the animal was slain, blood was smeared on the horn of the altar of burnt offerings, the rest of the blood was poured at the base of the altar, the fat of the animal was burned, and the rest was either taken outside of the camp or eaten by the priests.

• Trespass Offerings (Lev 5:14-6:7)

Trespass offerings are closely related to sin offerings, except these include sins related to the injury of another individual. We are given three specific instances where trespass offerings would be given: sin concerning the holy laws of the Lord [5:14-16], sin concerning the violating of commandments [5:17-19], and sin concerning cases of moral fraud (stealing, lying, etc.) [6:1-7].

Feasts and Festivals

Chapter seven of Leviticus discusses the Priests' specific roles in administering the sacrifices. In conjunction with these sacrifices, God commanded the Israelites to observe certain feasts and festivals. These events are listed below with brief summaries.

• The Day of Atonement (Lev 16:1-34)

The Day of Atonement was one of the most important days observed by Israel. This day is also called Yom Kippur and it occurs on the tenth day of the seventh month (around the end of September). After Nadab and Abihu offered a sacrifice with strange fire [16:1-2], the Lord instructed Aaron to enter the Most Holy Place once a year. This act by Aaron was to make atonement, not just for the sins of the people, but for the whole nation of Israel (priests and physical sanctuaries included). This day was a complete cleansing of the camp of God, but it only lasted for one year; this day had to be observed year after year. The nation of Israel was to offer sacrifices on that day, keep a strict fast, and not do any work.

• The Sabbath (Lev 23:1-3)

The Sabbath day was the most frequent and well-known holy day, as it occurred every week and was mentioned in the Ten Commandments. The Sabbath was a day of rest every seventh day, which was to remind the people of God's deliverance from oppression and slavery (Deut 5:15). The seventh day of rest reminded them of God's day of resting when He created the world (Ex 20:11). The day was to be a day of "holy convocation" [23:3], which meant a holy assembly was gathered together to fulfill specific duties expressed by God.

• The Day of New Moons (Num 28:11-15)

The next most frequent holy day was the Day of New Moons. Not much was said of this day, but David mentioned this special day in 1 Samuel 20. The Day of New Moons occurred every first day of the new month and called for the people to offer additional sacrifices on that day.

• Passover Feast and Day of Unleavened Bread (Lev 23:4-14)

The Passover and Day of Unleavened Bread were yearly feasts that helped the Israelites remember the night when God passed over the homes during the tenth plague on Egypt. The Passover feast occurred on the first month of the Jewish calendar, followed immediately by a seven-day feast of eating unleavened bread. These days helped focus the minds of God's people back to when He provided for them during both the tenth plague and the wilderness wanderings.

• The Feast of Pentecost (Lev 23:15-22)

The term "Pentecost" was not specifically used in the Old Testament, but was a term the Greeks used in the New Testament. Other names for this feast were: Feast of Weeks (Ex 34:22), Feast of Harvest (Ex 23:16), Day of Firstfruits (Num 28:26), and Feast of the Fifty Days (as used by Josephus). This day occurred fifty days after Passover, thus the Greek name Pentecost. This day is significant in that the events in Acts 2 occur during the time of Pentecost. A large majority of Jews would have made the journey to Jerusalem for Passover and stayed an additional fifty days for Pentecost.

• The Seventh Month (Lev 23:23-44)

The seventh month of the Jewish calendar was a significant month as many events occurred then. For example, the Day of Atonement occurred during this month. The Feast of Trumpets was a special New Moon feast, where emphasis was placed on the first day of the seventh month. The other large event was the Feast of Tabernacles, which was a seven-day engagement where special sacrifices were made. This feast in particular marked the end of the harvest season. Individuals were to leave their homes and make tents (hence the term "tabernacle") to remember the wilderness wanderings.

• The Sabbatical Year (Lev 25:1-7)

On the seventh year, God's people were not to plant any crops on the land...a picture of God's land having a year of rest. The Israelites had to rely on the crops they harvested for the six years leading up to the Sabbath year. During this seventh year, many other significant events transpired: Hebrew slaves were set free (Deut 15:12-18), Hebrew debts to other Hebrews were released (Deut 15:1-11), and the Old Law was read aloud to the entire assembly (Deut 31:9-13).

• The Year of Jubilee (Lev 25:8-55)

Every fiftieth year was a Year of Jubilee where property sold to others was given back to their original owners, signifying the people were "renting" the land from the Lord [25:10]. Property and slaves were returned for a fair value [25:15f]. This fiftieth year was to be a year of celebration, a remembering of the blessings from God, and a reminder that God "rented" His land to the people [25:23]. During this Year of Jubilee, the Lord promised to provide for Israelites and care for their needs [15:18-22].

DRAWING OUT **DEEPER MEANINGS**

Sin Offerings: Concessions for the Poor

In Leviticus 5:7-13 we see exceptions were made for those who were poor and could not afford a goat or lamb. If an individual could not afford the animal, they could bring two turtledoves or pigeons. One was to be used as the sin offering and the other to be used as the burnt offering after the first was offered. If an individual could not afford the birds, they were permitted to use half a gallon of flour instead. Why is this important to note? This concession helps explain why Jesus' family did what they did in Luke 2:22-24 when they offered a sacrifice of turtledoves or pigeons in Jerusalem.

The Number Seven

The number seven is used quite a bit in the scriptures, often in a symbolic way. Books such as Daniel and Revelation use the number in their apocalyptic style of literature. In discussing the feasts and festivals, the number seven is significant in a variety of ways:

• The Sabbath Day occurred every seventh day, and the Sabbath Year every seventh year.
• The seventh Sabbath Year was followed by a Year of Jubilee.
• Every seventh month was a holy month, consisting of three different feasts.
• The Passover Feast lasted seven days and there were seven weeks between Passover and Pentecost.
• During Passover, fourteen lambs (two sevens) were offered daily.
• During the Feast of Tabernacles, fourteen lambs (two sevens) were offered daily, as well as seventy (ten sevens) bulls during the feast.
• During Pentecost, seven lambs were offered.

DRAWING OUT **TAKE AWAYS**

Three things you should remember after reviewing this lesson:

1. Should We Observe Old Testament Feasts Today?

The Sabbath was a special rest day for God's people. It was to be observed every seventh day, with a special Sabbath Year on the seventh year. Many wonder if we should observe the Sabbath law or any of the other feasts/ festivals today. In helping answer this question, we must look to what God says through the New Testament. Hebrews 4 indicates there is a greater Sabbath coming, possibly telling us that the Sabbath of the Old Law is void. Furthermore, Colossians 2 tells us something very important about the Old Testament feasts and festivals: these regulations and special days were only a shadow of something with more substance – Christ (Col 2:16f). The Old Testament way of life is not binding on us today as Christians, but shows us a complete picture of God's scheme of redemption, pointing the way to Christ as the ultimate fulfillment of these feasts and festivals.

2. Christ and the Day of Atonement

The Day of Atonement is a type and foreshadow of Christ. We see certain points of comparison with the Day of Atonement and Christ's sacrifice. Aaron, who was called to perform the actions of a high priest (much like Christ was called), had to purify himself by putting on a white royal garment and offering a sin offering for himself. Christ prepared the way for our atonement by purifying himself – in perfect righteousness and holiness – not needing a sin offering to cleanse Him. Aaron, as the high priest, had to enter into the Most Holy Place once a year to make atonement for sin, where Christ was able to enter into heaven once (Heb 9:24) and make one sacrifice that lasted a lifetime (Heb 10:19-22). The blood of Jesus was taken into the Most Holy Place (i.e., heaven) for a once-for-all atonement for sin. The Day of Atonement and the whole Old Testament sacrificial system is inferior to the system of Christ because: the priests had to offer sacrifices for their own sins unlike Christ (Lev 16:11), the blood of bulls and goats could not atone for sins (Heb 10:4), and the sacrifices and Day of Atonement were to be offered daily/yearly (Heb 7:25f). Jesus Christ is the perfect solution for everyone, Jew or Gentile.

3. The Passover Lamb of Christ

When we look at the Passover, there are many connections to Jesus Christ. The New Testament tells us Jesus has acted as our "passover lamb" by sacrificing himself (1 Cor 5:7). On Passover, the Jews made sure all leaven was out of their homes. In comparison, we need to remove all leaven of sin since our Passover lamb has been sacrificed (1 Cor 5:1-11). Similar to the Passover lamb in that its bones were not broken, we remember that Christ's bones were also unbroken (Ex 12:46; John 19:36). The Passover symbolized Israel's deliverance from the Egyptians and our Passover lamb helps us remember our deliverance from the bondage of sin when we eat the Lord's Supper (John 8:30-34; Rom 3:23). Jesus truly was the ultimate fulfillment of the Passover and we are blessed to remember the great sacrifice that was made for all mankind.

DRAWING OUT **THOUGHT QUESTIONS**

1. What shadows of the Passover do you see fulfilled in Christ and the church? _____

_____

_____

_____

2. Is the Sabbath "forever" (Ex 31:16f)? Are we supposed to observe the Sabbath today (Heb 7:11f; 9:10)? _____

_____

_____

_____

3. Is it true that Sunday is the New Testament "Christian Sabbath?" ____

_____

_____

_____

4. Could the Old Testament sacrifices themselves remove sin? What was their purpose? Were sins forgiven in the Old Testament? _____

_____

_____

_____

5. How did these feasts, festivals, and sacrifices make God's people more holy? _____

_____

_____

_____

LESSON TWELVE

THE TABERNACLE

Exodus 25-27, 30-31, 35-40

DRAWING OUT **HIGHLIGHTS**

- God gives Moses detailed instructions on how to build the Tabernacle, a dwelling place for Him as the people continued to travel
- The Tabernacle is constructed in a particular way and has a variety of furnishings that are specified by God
- The Tabernacle has various laws and rules surrounding it, including who is authorized to enter it, when, and for what purpose

DRAWING OUT **CONTEXT**

The Tabernacle plan was revealed to Moses when he was on Mount Sinai. It was a portable tent that was moved from place to place as the Israelites traveled. The Tabernacle was the central place of worship in the days of Moses up until the days of Solomon (c. 970 BC). How was the Tabernacle funded? It was not from taxation, but rather from Israelite freewill offerings [25:1-9]. This money was in the form of gold, silver, cloth, skins, oils, spices, stones, etc. God instructed Moses on what should be included in the Tabernacle and how each element should be constructed [25-27].
Here are some highlights of what God specified about His tabernacle:

Ark of the Covenant (Ex 25:10-15)

The Ark was made of wood and overlaid with pure gold. There were four rings on top where staves were placed so the Levites could carry it from place to place. The Ark was a symbol of God and His law...which should be at the center of the people's hearts. There were three items placed in the Ark: a gold pot of manna (which represented God's physical providence),

Tabernacle Diagram

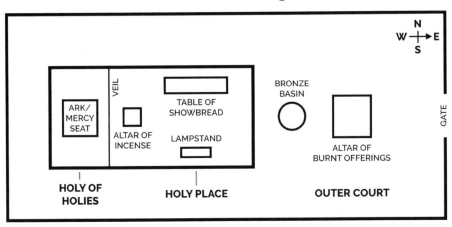

Aaron's rod that budded (which represented God's choice in priesthood), and the tablets of the Law (which represented God's commands in the covenant). These three items were important because they were "interconnected" – to change one was to change the others. For example, if the priesthood had changed (Heb 7:12) then so would the Law and the covenant (cf. Jer 31; Heb 8).

Mercy Seat (Ex 25:17-22)

The Mercy Seat was a solid gold lid that was placed on top of the Ark of the Covenant. There were two cherubim made of gold whose wings covered the Mercy Seat. It was here that the Lord said, "There will I meet with you, and from above the Mercy Seat...I will speak with you" [25:22].

Table of Showbread (Ex 25:23-30)

The Table of Showbread was a wooden table overlaid with gold. Golden rings were attached to it with staves so it could be easily transported. The purpose of the table was to be a constant memorial, acknowledgment, and reminder of God's goodness in physically providing for the people.

Golden Lampstand (Ex 25:31-40)

This object was made of pure gold, not molded but beaten. There was one central lamp with six branches coming off of it, for a total of seven places for lights. This lampstand was used for actual lighting, but also symbolized the "light" of God's truth. It also paralleled the Israelites' "light" that was supposed to shine to all the nations of the earth.

Layout of the Tabernacle (Ex 26)

The Tabernacle consisted of multiple parts. The first part mentioned was an inner tent, which was a thin fabric that was the first layer of covering over the Tabernacle. The second was an outer tent made from goat hair. This provided protection from weather elements and it was placed on top of the inner tent covering. The Tabernacle was to have exterior walls made of wooden boards constructed in such a way they could easily be dismantled. A veil was then instructed to be made, separating the Tabernacle into two sections: the Holy Place and the Holy of Holies. This veil was made of blue, purple, and scarlet twined linen. The Holy Place contained the Table of Showbread, the Golden Lampstand, and the Altar of Incense. The Holy of Holies contained the Ark of the Covenant.

Outer Court (Ex 27:9-19)

The Outer Court was made to separate the actual Tabernacle from worldly affairs. The sides of the court were made from thin linen curtains.

Bronze Altar (Ex 27:1-8)

The Bronze Altar, also called the Altar of Burnt Offerings, was placed in the outer court that surrounded the Holy Place and the Holy of Holies. It was at this altar where sacrifices that atoned for sins were offered.

Oil for Lampstand (Ex 27:20f)

The oil that the Lord commanded to be used was pure olive oil, which allowed the lampstand to continue burning bright. The lampstand was to have enough olive oil so as to light the Tabernacle continually throughout the night.

Altar of Incense (Ex 30:1-10)

The Altar of Incense was placed just before the veil that separated the Holy of Holies from the Holy Place. It was gold-plated with horns on the altar and rings that had staves used for transportation. Incense was burned every morning and evening, and once a year blood was sprinkled on it during the Day of Atonement.

Bronze Basin (Ex 30:17-21)

The Basin, also called the Laver, contained water used for ceremonial washings and purifications for the priests since washing was required before anyone entered the Tabernacle. It was made of solid brass or bronze, and a violation of not washing in the way God commanded was punishable by death.

DRAWING OUT **DEEPER MEANINGS**

Typology in the Bible

Symbols in the Bible are often referred to as 'types' while the greater elements they represent are referred to as the 'antitypes.' Together this is known as biblical typology. For example, according to 1 Peter 3, we see Noah/the flood was a type of something greater; the antitype is baptism/ the removal of sins. The underlying assumption in typology is that God is in control of history, seen in the fact that these types and antitypes are no accident or coincidence. In God's scheme of redemption, He has designed events of one age to serve as a "shadow" of things to come in another age (cf. Heb 10:1). Many, however, misunderstand the unifying purpose of types and antitypes; it is a mistake to think of typology as only "Old Testament shadows of New Testament realities." Rather, the unifying purpose of typology is to show heavenly realities from earthly shadows. This is because both the Old and New Testaments (i.e., not just the Old Testament alone) have types and antitypes that refer to a reality greater than something here on earth. The Tabernacle is an example of a type that has antitypes in the New Testament (i.e., in the age of Christ) and beyond (i.e., Heaven) and even has shadows that reach back before the Mosaic Covenant.

Freedom and Specific Commands

It can be daunting to review all the chapters of Exodus and read the multiple, very specific commands God had for the construction of the Tabernacle. It is obvious, however, when you read the text that God had a particular way He wanted the Tabernacle built [25:9,40]. Did that leave room for the Israelites to make any changes they thought would be better? There is a very important principle concerning communication we need to consider: the more specific a request is, the less freedom we have. On the flip side, the more general or generic a request is, the more freedom we have. This is not just some "biblical interpretation method," but rather a universal principle in communication. For example, if you are asked to get a Pepsi, but you bring back a Sprite instead, you have not fulfilled the specific request. However, if you are asked to get a soda and you bring back a Sprite (or a Pepsi...or any carbonated beverage), you would have fulfilled the generic request. God gave Moses and the Israelites many commands and it was clear that the Tabernacle's specific instructions did not leave room for personal discretion. The same could be said for the specific instructions regarding Noah's ark.

DRAWING OUT **TAKE AWAYS**

Three things you should remember after reviewing this lesson:

1. "Tabernacles" Throughout the Scheme of Redemption

While the word "tabernacle" simply refers to a tent or dwelling place, the Bible espouses a sacredness to the term. In the Old Testament, the idea of a tabernacle often refers to the housing, dwelling, or glory of God. The story of the Bible begins with God "tabernacling" with man in the Garden of Eden; God and man living together in perfect harmony. Sin enters the world and then a separation has to be made. The theme of the Bible can be summarized in how God makes it again possible for His people to dwell with Him. In the Law of Moses, God allows a limited dwelling place for Himself among the people via the Tabernacle. When Solomon built the Temple, God's glory "moved in" and dwelt with the people in a more permanent way. But when God's people rebelled, they were carried off into captivity, the city of Jerusalem was destroyed, and God's glory left the Temple. It did not return when the second temple was built by Zerubbabel, but came back to dwell with man in the most unlikely way... in the form of a human. God "tabernacled" with man through Christ and would institute a new way in which God's glory would dwell with all of mankind who believe. However, Christ – the man – died on the cross... so where does God's glory dwell now? The dwelling of God does not reside in a temple made with hands, but a new temple, open for both Jew and Gentile. This new "tabernacle" is seen in the church, which in itself is a type of something greater (the antitype being Heaven). The only way to dwell in the presence of God is through His church, where God "tabernacles" with man today. Through Christ's church we can all be a part of the kingdom of God and eventually dwell with Him in Heaven where God will ultimately "tabernacle" with man for eternity.

2. Christ as the Mercy Seat of God

In describing the Mercy Seat, God said, "There will I meet with you" [25:22]. The Mercy Seat is translated from a word which means "to cover." The idea here is that God covered the people with His presence and glory. It also represents God's mercy for the people as He covered the Ark of the Covenant...reminding them that only He can atone for transgressions of the Law that's contained within. The concept of the Mercy Seat continues in the New Testament in Hebrews 9:5 and we see it tied directly to Christ in Romans 3:25 where Paul says, "Christ was put forward by God to be a propitiation by His blood." What is propitiation? This word comes from the Greek word 'hilasterion,' which is often translated as "mercy seat." This passage, as well as 1 John 2:2 and 4:10, tell us that Christ is performing the functions of the Mercy Seat! It is through Christ that God covers us with His presence, glory, and mercy.

3. The Then Limited Accessibility of God

While we have already established that the Tabernacle provided a way for God to dwell with His people, His accessibility was limited to a large degree. The author of Hebrews says that, "The way into the Most Holy Place had not yet been shown while the first Tabernacle was standing" (Heb 9:8). The design and regulation of the Tabernacle offered the

Israelites only the most limited kind of access to God. In other words, God was inaccessible and off-limits to the average Israelite. Most people were barred from coming into the Most Holy of Holies, which housed the Ark of the Covenant and the Mercy Seat (where God's glory dwelt among His people). This Holy of Holies was separated by a veil. If the Tabernacle is an earthly symbol of a heavenly meaning, then one can reason that we are separated from the presence of God! The amazing thing for us is that Christ "tore the curtain of the Temple in two from top to bottom" (Matt 27:51) and He now appears in the presence of God on our behalf (Heb 9:24). What does that mean? The only way that we can be in the presence of God is through Jesus Christ, who acts as our mediator and High Priest.

DRAWING OUT **THOUGHT QUESTIONS**

1. How did Moses raise funds to complete the Tabernacle? Why might this be significant? _____

_____

_____

_____

2. According to Exodus 40:33f, what had to happen before the glory of God could enter the Tabernacle? _____

_____

_____

_____

3. Use passages in Hebrews chapter nine to show how the Tabernacle was a 'type' of something greater. _____

_____

_____

_____

4. From what cardinal direction did an individual enter the Tabernacle? What
   other biblical location might that remind you of? How might that location and
   the Tabernacle be related? _____

   _____

   _____

   _____

5. What are some examples of discretions and absolutes we have/find when
   looking at the generic and specific commands in the New Law? _____

   _____

   _____

   _____

PRIESTS AND LEVITES

Exodus 28-29, Leviticus 7-10, 21-22, Numbers 3-4, 8, 18

DRAWING OUT **HIGHLIGHTS**

- God selects Aaron and his sons to be priests, making Aaron the first high priest
- Offering sacrifices on behalf of the people is one of the priests' main duties
- The Levites have special responsibilities to the Lord as another group of His chosen people
- God gives specific instructions as to the wardrobe the priests would wear

DRAWING OUT **CONTEXT**

The Old Law ushered in both new social and religious orders for God's people. The establishment of the priesthood was one such order. Moses was instructed by God to ordain Aaron and his family line from the tribe of Levi as priests, serving the rest of God's people. Aaron, and then the first-born of his descendants, could be designated as high priests who had special responsibilities in service to the people [Ex 28:1]. The Levites themselves were also a chosen tribe of God, selected to render assistance to the priests and people [Num 8:15f]. Priests were easily recognized by their outfits, which were also designated by God [Ex 28:4ff]. While the Old Testament contains numerous accounts, aspects, and descriptions of the priests (and Levites) in Exodus, Leviticus, and Numbers, below are a few highlights of their responsibilities and wardrobe:

Levites

Members of this tribe who were not descendants of Aaron (i.e., not priests) would render service to the priests and help as needed. They would assist in dealing with tithes/offerings, in the teaching of the law, acting as the nation's scribes, regulators and judges, and in maintaining the places of worship. The Levites contributed a lot to the people of Israel and to the priests they helped and served. A Levite would initially begin his service at the age of twenty-five and continue through age fifty (Num 8:24).

Priests

The consecration of the priests is seen in Exodus 29, which includes washings, anointings, sin offerings, burnt offerings, peace offerings, the consecration of the altar, and more. It's clear in this chapter that God is setting any and everything apart – cleansing it – for its involvement in worship or appearance in His presence. The priests served the main function of offering the people's sacrifices to God. They were mediators between God and His people. They could also intercede and inquire of God on behalf of the people. Additional rules and regulations for the priests are found in Leviticus 21:1-9, 16-24.

High Priests

The high priest was considered the "religious leader" of the Israelites. Only the first-born from the line of Aaron was eligible to become a high priest. As the leader, the high priest was to oversee the other priests in their service (cf. 2 Cor 19:11). As a priest himself, the high priest was to perform all of the functions as a priest, but there were certain responsibilities and privileges reserved only for the high priest. As an example, only the high priest wore the Urim and Thummim, which was a way to inquire of God's will on a subject. In the matter of sacrifices, the high priest offered sacrifices for the sins of all the people and for himself, too. On the Day of Atonement, it was only the high priest who was allowed to enter the Holy of Holies and stand before God and offer a sacrifice for the last year's sins committed by the people. Additional rules and regulations for the priests are found in Leviticus 21:10-15. Interestingly enough, whenever a high priest died, those who had sought asylum in the cities of refuge for manslaughter were granted freedom (Num 35:28).

Priestly Garments

In Exodus 28 the detailed description of the clothing God prescribed priests to wear is listed. The clothing's purpose was to set the priests apart from the rest of God's people. The outfits featured:

• Ephod (Ex 28:6-14) – a shawl or wrap made of blue, purple, and scarlet linen. Golden shoulder clasps were also used. The waistband consisted of the same linens.

• Breastplate (Ex 28:15-30) – a pouch made of woven material with twelve stones on it (four rows of three) that had the twelve tribes of Israel engraved on them. The pouch was designed to hold the Urim and Thummim. The breastplate was held up by golden chains and blue ribbons that attached it to the ephod.

• Robe (Ex 28:31-35) – a robe made of blue cloth with gold bells and embroidered pomegranates around its hem. The sound of the bells indicated God's presence to Aaron when he entered/left the Holy Place.

• Turban (Ex 28:36-38) – a headpiece made of linen with a gold plate in front. "Holy to the Lord" was engraved on the plate, which symbolized the guilt of the people on the high priest's head.

• Other Garments (Ex 28:39-43) – these include an embroidered sash and the undergarments.

The outfit was not optional; it had to be worn. God says in Exodus 28:43, "Aaron and his sons must wear [the outfits] whenever they enter the tent of meeting or approach the altar to minister in the Holy Place, so that they will not incur guilt and die."

DRAWING OUT **DEEPER MEANINGS**

The Difficult Work of Priests and Levites

It's one thing to say that "the priests just offered sacrifices for the people" and it's another to read about the amount of work priests had to perform. Their job was to not only minister to the Lord, but to the people. Their service to the Lord was manifested in their many responsibilities, including daily offerings, the burning of incense, tending to the lamps on the lampstand, and the weekly renewal of bread. Their service to the people included their attendance at all the tabernacle sacrifices and catching the blood as the animals died (which they then offered and ate the portions assigned to the priests). The Levites also had many responsibilities. They were the ones who set up and took down the tabernacle, prepared it for transport, and moved the Ark and other furnishings. What was the pay these workers received? Numbers 18 tells us that the priests and Levites were actually not going to receive any inheritance in the promised land. Instead, their payment was the tithes offered by the people. The tithes (and some portions of offerings) were given to the priests to support themselves; their work was paying them back in a sense. Paul makes this point in 1 Corinthians 9:13f when mentioning the fact that those who serve the Lord and people today – preachers – should be supported. Paul says, "Don't you know that those who serve in the temple get their food from the temple, and that those who serve at the altar share in what is offered on the altar? In the same way, the Lord has commanded that those who preach the gospel should receive their living from the gospel." After a thorough look at their responsibilities seen throughout the Old Testament, the work of a priest and Levite was not easy, and it should not be said that anyone who works in service to the Lord (even a preacher today) has an easy task before him.

Priests Were Partakers at the Altar

After the death of Nadab and Abihu in Leviticus 10, we find Aaron and his sons (Eleazar and Ithamar) in shock over what has happened. It appears they were in so much shock they neglected to fully complete the sacrifice they offered as prescribed by God, which required them to eat part of the offering. This was a duty of the priests and Moses was concerned about them forsaking this portion of the offering...especially after what had just happened [Lev 10:17f]. While Moses dropped his inquiry after hearing Aaron's response [Lev 10:19], it is interesting to note that one of the important parts of the priestly duties was to indeed partake of some of the offering when performing certain sacrifices. The atonement came through the priest eating a portion of those sacrifices. This is a perfect parallel to the sacrifice that was given on our behalf –Jesus. We must "partake" in the sacrifice as "priests" in order to be atoned. Paul makes this point in 1 Corinthians 10:16, 18 when he says, "Is not the cup of thanksgiving for which we give thanks a participation in the blood of Christ? And is not the bread that we break a participation in the body of Christ?...Consider the people of Israel: Do not those who eat the sacrifices participate in the altar?" So when the priests offered sacrifices on behalf of the people, let us remember that they too were intimately involved in partaking of the actual sacrifice, which was the only way God would then atone His people for their transgressions.

DRAWING OUT **TAKE AWAYS**

Three things you should remember after reviewing this lesson:

1. Christians are a Royal Priesthood

Out of God's already chosen people, the priests were another subset given great privileges. The priests specifically offered sacrifices to God that the average person could not. After Jesus died on the cross and became the perfect sacrifice for sin (Heb 10:12), there was no longer a need for sacrifices under the Old Law nor priests required to offer them. Under the New Law, Christians are "priests" and today we can offer spiritual sacrifices to God. Just as God called the priests to serve in this manner, He has also chosen another group of people – Christians – to do the same. In 1 Peter 2:5-9 we read, "You also, as living stones, are being built up a spiritual house, a holy priesthood, to offer up spiritual sacrifices acceptable to God through Jesus Christ...But you are a chosen generation, a royal priesthood, a holy nation, His own special people, that you may proclaim the praises of Him who called you out of darkness into His marvelous light." Here Peter makes it clear Christians are the "new priesthood" and the sacrifices we offer are spiritual. Why is this important? Because under the Old Law, only the high priest could go into the Holy of Holies (i.e., come before God), but under the New Law, Jesus is our high priest and Christians now have that same, direct access to God without the need of an earthly priest.

2. Our "Priestly Garments"

The priests in the Old Testament were given great responsibilities and put in a place of honor among God's people. A priest was recognizable due to his appearance/outfit. The priestly garments were set in place by God to show that these individuals were set apart for a special purpose. Onlookers could tell just by seeing that they didn't blend in with the rest of the normally-dressed crowd. Some portions of their wardrobe had special functions and purposes as designed by God (e.g., a pouch for the Urim and Thummim, the gold bells, etc). As Christians, we too are set apart from the rest of the world as God's people. While we don't have an outfit to demonstrate that, our actions on the outside should show others what's on our inside and make it obvious that we do not "blend in with the crowd." We are set apart for a purpose. Furthermore, while we don't have special functions within a wardrobe (let alone a wardrobe at all), Paul tells us in Ephesians 6:10-18 that we have spiritual armor we must wear, and it too has special functions. Today we can "wear" the helmet of salvation, the breastplate of righteousness, the belt of truth, and carry with us the shield of faith and the sword of the Spirit.

3. Don't Offer "Strange Fire"

We read in Leviticus 10 and Numbers 3 that Nadab and Abihu offered incense with "strange fire" and were killed because of it. Remember, all the instructions and commands regarding offerings were clearly outlined for them. While we don't know what the "strange fire" was, we do know it was unauthorized and profane; God rejected it because it did not sanctify Him. Two suggested possibilities for this "strange fire" include them (1) not using the proper fire from the altar (cf. Lev 19:12) and (2) entering the Tabernacle drunk, being careless, and forgetting or neglecting God's instructions (cf. Lev 10:8f). God struck them as a sign and as an example that He must be sanctified and worship offered to Him must be given only on His terms. Today, we must expect the same response from God – He does not accept worship that is unauthorized and profane or offered with the wrong attitude and heart. The Lord asks the rhetorical question in Malachi 1:8 when He says, "When you offer blind animals for sacrifice, is that not wrong? When you sacrifice lame or diseased animals, is that not wrong? Try offering them to your governor! Would he be pleased with you? Would he accept you?" It's clear that if man won't even accept something that he didn't specifically request, why would God be any different? We need to remember that while God is a loving God, He is not a God that will simply let everything slide; He must be worshiped and approached in the correct manner or else there will be consequences.

DRAWING OUT **THOUGHT QUESTIONS**

1. What role(s) did the high priest specifically play in offerings on the Day of Atonement? Hint: Leviticus 16. _____

_____

_____

_____

2. Why do many denominations have priests today? What is their purpose today? _____

_____

_____

_____

3. What are some parallels we find in the high priest's roles/responsibilities/ privileges under the Old Law and those of our high priest, Jesus Christ's?

_____

_____

_____

_____

4. What was the significance of the priestly garments? Is there any significance to religious outfits worn by many in the religious world today? _____

_____

_____

_____

5. Nadab and Abihu were made an example of by God (by their deaths) because of their disobedience. What couple was also made an example of by God (also by their deaths) in the New Testament? How do the sins in both accounts relate to correctly offering/sacrificing to God? _____

_____

_____

_____

_____

LESSON FOURTEEN
MISCELLANEOUS LAWS

Exodus 21-23; Leviticus 11-15, 17-20, 27

DRAWING OUT **HIGHLIGHTS**

- God gives specific and detailed laws regarding a variety of civil and social circumstances while Moses was on Mount Sinai
- The purpose of the laws is to keep the people holy and set apart

DRAWING OUT **CONTEXT**

When we read about the various aspects of the Old Law, we must understand that all the commandments in the law are based upon the Ten Commandments, although there are many ways to categorize all the commandments in the law. In this lesson we have combined commands from Exodus 21-23 and Leviticus 11-15, 17-20, 27 into a single grouping of "miscellaneous laws." These laws cover topics including civil trials and justice, treatment of enemies and foreigners, sexual sins and adultery, child sacrifices, and more. The laws in this lesson might seem random, but they all serve a common purpose: to transform the Israelites into a holy people. We will not look at every law given in these sections, but will highlight a few:

Laws Regarding Slavery (Ex 21:1-11)

An Israelite could become a slave either voluntarily through poverty (Lev 25:35-45) or involuntarily through criminal action [Ex 22:3]. Slavery typically lasted for six years, unless specific situations dictated otherwise. Laws Regarding Capital Punishment (Ex 21:12-17)

The punishment for murder was always death, but an accidental death did not call for the death penalty. Instead, the individual was to flee to one of the six cities of refuge God set up (Joshua 20), where he or she would then be judged. Striking one's parents, either physically or verbally, was a capital offense punishable by death.

Laws Regarding Bodily Injury (Ex 21:18-32)

Laws were given regarding injuries that happened to and from various parties: fighting among brethren, injury to servants, injury to pregnant women, and injury from ox goring. The basic concept introduced here is "an eye is required for the injury of an eye" [21:23f].

Laws Regarding Uncleanness (Lev 11-15)

God also gave specific regulations for food, childbirth, and diseases. These are found primarily in Leviticus 11-15. These laws might seem arbitrary, but they had the specific purpose of helping the people be holy as God is holy [11:45]. Many people have tried to explain these laws as God giving medical help, advice, and good practices for His people. Although that is partially why these laws were in effect (cf. Ex 15:26), the main purpose of these commands was to stress the importance of holy living.

Laws Regarding Sacrifices (Lev 17:1-9)

God, in His ultimate foreknowledge and wisdom, regulated how animals were to be sacrificed. The people could not sacrifice any animal wherever he or she pleased; it had to be sacrificed in the way God ordained and at the proper location.

Laws Regarding the Eating of Blood (Lev 17:10-16)

The law forbade an Israelite to eat an animal that still had blood contained in it. This was not a new command, as Noah was given this same command in Genesis 9:4. When one of God's people slew an animal to eat, they had to bleed the animal properly before consuming its meat.

Laws Regarding Sexuality and the Marriage Covenant (Lev 18)

God's people were expected to be different from all the nations around them, and that included marriage and sexual relations. In summary, the Israelites were to follow the commands of the Lord and not imitate their neighbors [18:2f]. God specified instructions on how His people were to conduct themselves in these relationships.

Laws About Vows (Lev 27)

The last chapter in Leviticus discusses the seriousness of vows, both made to other people or to the Lord. This section might seem random to put at the end of the book, but it acts like an appendix of sorts. Topics in this section include vows made to a person, vows containing animals, vows containing houses, vows containing land, and things that are/are not supposed to be vowed to God.

Miscellaneous Laws (Lev 19)

In this section God lays out miscellaneous sundry laws that are tied to holy conduct. These laws are introduced by the Lord, reminding the people to "be holy for I am holy." There are twenty-eight different commands given by God in this section, with variety and in no particular order.

These laws and regulations were to be taken seriously by God's people; God gave punishments for any violations of these ordinances (Lev 20). These punishments were not given because God was being cruel, but rather to stress holy and righteous living in the hearts of His people. The promise of God's wrath for violations was just as strong as God's promise of care and protection for His people.

DRAWING OUT **DEEPER MEANINGS**

Thirty Pieces of Silver and Judas Iscariot

In Exodus 21:32, we read that a penalty was paid to the owner if his slave was gored and killed by an ox. The price was thirty pieces of silver.

That amount equated to about four months of wages for a laborer. We remember that Judas betrayed Jesus, but do we remember the amount Judas was paid? Thirty pieces of silver (Matt 26:15). The amount that Judas accepted to betray his Savior was not a million dollars or even enough to buy a new house or car. Rather, it was only thirty pieces of silver – the same amount you would pay someone if your bull killed a slave. Those thirty pieces of silver were used to betray our Savior, which ultimately provided us the perfect sacrifice that freed us from the slavery of sin.

Lex Talionis: An Eye For an Eye

'Lex Talionis' is the Latin term for the law of equal retribution, where the punishment resembles the offense committed to the same degree. In other words, it is an "eye for an eye and a tooth for a tooth." God's Old Law centered around this concept...not to promote personal vengeance, but fair justice. Lex Talionis is a major theme of the Bible and we see glimpses of it throughout scripture. We clearly see this idea in Exodus 21-24: transgressions deserve equal punishment. The concept of Lex Talionis is continued even into the New Law, because we all have sinned and deserve equal punishment (Rom 3:23).

Greater Understanding of the New Testament

We read about the things that make an Israelite clean/unclean in Leviticus 11-20. This was important to help keep God's people separate and distinct from the foreign nations around them. Reading and understanding the laws of uncleanness help us better understand many New Testament passages. Below are some chapters on uncleanness and some New Testament passages that correspond to those specific laws:

- Eating Animals: Leviticus 11 – Mark 7; Acts 10
- Childbirth: Leviticus 12 – Luke 2:22-24
- Leprosy: Leviticus 13-14 – Mark 1:40-45
- Eating Blood: Leviticus 17 – Acts 15:22-29; Hebrews 10:29-34
- Homosexuality: Leviticus 18 – 1 Corinthians 6:9-11

DRAWING OUT **TAKE AWAYS**

Three things you should remember after reviewing this lesson:

1. The Deadly Price of Sin

The concept of 'Lex Talionis' is continued into the New Law in that we deserve equal punishment for our sins...and we're told the wages of sin is death. Romans 3:23 says we're all guilty when Paul writes, "We all sin and fall short of the glory of God." But we now know a more "advanced principle," realizing that Christ came to save us from this curse of death (cf. Gal 4:1-7). Christ became the propitiation for sin, and this was the plan all along. This was the "advanced principle" that the Jews in Paul's day could not understand. With Christ, we can move past the elementary principles, understand the advanced ones, and fully understand the big picture.

2. The Nature of the Mosaic Covenant

It is important to understand that the covenant was a law code, a two-party contractual agreement that elevated God's people over all the other nations, conditional on obedience. The law set up a completely different lifestyle than those of foreign nations, and even the "wilderness wandering" lifestyle of God's own people. God's people were soon to be tenants of the Lord's land and needed a law to establish and regulate how they were supposed to live in that land. The longer God's people wandered in the wilderness, the less important and relevant the law seemed to the people. When we hear God's Old Law preached, often times specific passages may not apply to our specific situations today. But we should not be like the Israelites and feel like God's Old Law is not important and relevant to us. More is said about the nature of the Old Law and how it relates to us today in lesson twenty-four.

3. "Be Holy For I Am Holy"

Holiness is the most emphasized characteristic of God in the Old Testament. In fact, one fifth of the total uses of the term 'holy' in the entire Bible occur in the book of Leviticus. Being holy means to sanctify or to set apart for a sacred purpose. In the New Testament, we know that Christians are to live holy (set apart) lives that are defined by a certain standard of conduct (cf. 1 Pet 1:13-19). It was the same with the Israelites. God's people were to be set apart and different by their conduct, appearance (inward and outward), and religious practices. God is unique, different, and set apart from other gods foreign nations worship. God's people should also be unique, different, and set apart from everyone else in the world. In other words, God's people are to be holy as He is holy [Lev 20:26].

DRAWING OUT **THOUGHT QUESTIONS**

1. How was God's law regarding slavery different from Egyptian slavery? Hint: Exodus 21:1-11; Leviticus 25:35-45. _____

_____

_____

_____

2. Why was the punishment for striking one's parents so severe? _____

_____

_____

_____

3. What was the purpose of God giving so many (seemingly strict) laws?

_____

_____

_____

4. What does it mean to be holy and how were God's people to put on holiness? _____

_____

_____

5. How is the Old Law relevant to us today as New Testament
Christians? _____

_____

_____

_____

LESSON FIFTEEN
LEAVING SINAI
Numbers 1-2; 10-12

DRAWING OUT **HIGHLIGHTS**

- Moses takes a census of the males (except from the tribe of Levi) over the age of twenty
- The Lord instructs the people on how they are to arrange the camp and where each tribe is to be placed in relation to the Tabernacle
- The Lord gives Moses assurance of His presence by providing a cloud to follow the people
- The Israelites complain about the journey and about the manna they are given to eat
- Miriam and Aaron challenge Moses' position of leadership

DRAWING OUT **CONTEXT**

The book of Numbers (and even whole books of the law) can be summarized by Numbers 1:1: "The Lord spoke to Moses." God had been communicating with Moses up on the mountain for quite some time (the Israelites were camped at Mount Sinai for about eleven months), but now God was communicating with Moses in preparation of leaving Mount Sinai. The first command we see in Numbers was for Moses to take a census of the males (except from the tribe of Levi) aged twenty and older [1:1-54]. Why just the males? Most likely because the Israelites were about to conquer the promised land and Moses was to take a census of "able and active soldiers" in God's army. The Lord assigned an individual from each tribe to help Moses in this process. The total number of males within the nation of Israel was 603,550. The Levites were not soldiers, but instead were to be camped around the Tabernacle, likely as stationed guards [1:53].

The Lord then instructed Moses on how the tribes should be arranged when they camp [2:1-34]. The Tabernacle should be in the middle of the camp, with the tribes arranged around it on four different sides. The eastern side of the camp included a "leader tribe" of Judah, with Issachar and Zebulun beside them. The southern side had the leader tribe of Reuben, along with Simeon and Gad. The western side had the leader tribe of Ephraim, along with Manasseh and Benjamin. The northern side had the leader tribe of Dan, along with Asher and Naphtali.

Before moving out, God reassured His people by letting them know His presence (via a cloud) would be with them when they remained stationary or when they moved [9:15-23]. The Lord instructed Moses to construct two silver trumpets which were to be used in summoning the congregation and as a signal to move out [10:1-10]. These trumpets were also to be used during special feasts and new moon festivals.

The journey could finally begin! Yet, only three days into the journey to the promised land, the Lord's people were found complaining again [11:1-3]. The Lord heard their complaining and sent fire down from heaven, but relented when Moses (yet again) intervened on behalf of the people. Not only did they complain about the travels, but the Israelites complained about the food situation to the point where individuals were weeping on their own doorsteps because all they had to eat was manna [11:4-35]. The Lord helped Moses deal with these difficult people by appointing seventy elders to assist Moses. The Lord also promised to punish the people by making them eat meat (quail) for a whole month. When the quail was gathered by the people, the Lord struck them with a great plague that killed many. Because of this event, the place was called Kibroth Hattaavah, which means "graves of lust" or "graves of greedinesses."

Moses led the people to Hazeroth and it is there that we read Moses married a Cushite woman [12:1-16]. Miriam and Aaron proceeded to criticize Moses and challenge his position of leadership, along with his special relationship with God. The Lord suddenly called Moses, Miriam, and Aaron together in the tent of meeting and made it very clear that Moses was a special servant who speaks to God in a special way: face-to-face. The Lord was angry at Miriam and Aaron, and struck Miriam with leprosy, making her unclean and an outcast of the camp for seven days. After Miriam was cured of her leprosy, the Israelites moved on from Hazeroth to the wilderness of Paran.

DRAWING OUT **DEEPER MEANINGS**

Why These Tribes on Those Sides of the Camp?

While the tribal order/placement in the camp might seem random, God had a purpose behind the arrangement. We know the side facing east was the front of the tabernacle, so God placed Judah, Issachar, and Zebulun on the eastern side of the camp. Judah was the biggest tribe of the Israelites (and arguably the more important), but not the oldest. Reuben was the oldest of the sons of Jacob, but was not given the place of "leader of the eastern side" of the Tabernacle because Reuben slept with his father's concubine. The second oldest son was Simeon, and he didn't receive the honor of leader of the eastern side because he attacked the Shechemites with Levi in Genesis 34. Judah, Issachar, and Zebulun were all sons of Leah, being the fourth, fifth, and sixth sons of Jacob. Reuben became the leader of the southern encampment, with Simeon and Gad, who were also sons of Leah. The western side of the camp included two of Joseph's sons, Ephraim and Manasseh, and Benjamin, who were all sons of Rachel. Dan was the leader of the northern side, because he was the oldest son of the concubine wives of Jacob, who also gave birth to Asher and Naphtali. The eastern and northern sides had the largest number of individuals, which shows the larger tribes carried the front and brought up the rear when they travelled. It may be easy to glance at this section of scripture and view it as random commands, but it is faith-building to see God's plan and purpose, even in such things as camp arrangements.

God is For and With His People

When the Israelites set out and marched they took the Ark of the Covenant with them. Whenever they lifted the Ark and set out to travel, Moses would proclaim, "Arise, O Lord, and let your enemies be scattered, and let those who hate you flee before you" [10:35]. Whenever the Israelites camped and rested the Ark, Moses would proclaim, "Return O Lord, to the ten thousand thousands of Israel" [10:36]. It is very clear Moses had zeal for the Lord, and initially, the people did too. Moses wanted to remind everyone in the congregation of two things: the Lord is (1) for them and the Lord is (2) with them. Today, when we feel like we cannot conquer our "enemies of the promised land," we need to remember that we are on the Lord's side, a side where He is both for and with us.

DRAWING OUT **TAKE AWAYS**

Three things you should remember after reviewing this lesson:

1. Why Does Zeal Fail?

It is interesting to see how excited the Israelites were when they began their journey into the promised land. Quickly, however, they became dissatisfied and rebelled against God by complaining. Their zeal was great at first, but the fire soon faded. Why was this the case? We often see the same reaction with new converts, who are on fire for the Lord the first months, but burnout soon and become discouraged. We need excitement with wisdom – zeal with discernment – and motivation with faith. Our journey as Christians is not like some extreme water sport (where we go about doing anything we want because we are excited, zealous, and we're in "open waters") allowing only our emotions and excited feelings to be our guide. Our excitement is to be expressed in a way that is led by the hand of God. In Matthew 14:22-33, Peter walked across the water with the help of Christ. Peter's zeal did not get him successfully across the water the first time, but once he grabbed hold of Christ's hand, he was able to cross. Zeal fails when it is not coupled with faith in God.

2. Excuses for Jealousy

We do not know much about the Cushite woman Moses married. It could have been a woman from the mixed multitude that went up from Egypt with the Israelites (cf. Ex 12:38). Possibly this multitude assimilated into the culture of the Jews and became Proselytes. Miriam and Aaron approached Moses soon after this marriage and doubted Moses. It is clear that the real point of contention was not the marriage of the Cushite woman, but was provoked from jealousy of Moses. This is indicated in Numbers 10:2

where they said, "Has the Lord spoken only to Moses? Has He not spoken to us also?" Miriam and Aaron were jealous of Moses' relationship with God and tried to cover it up with the excuse of the Cushite marriage. Often times we may become jealous or commit another sinful act, yet try to cover it up and find a scapegoat for it. We must take an honest look at our actions, thoughts, and hearts and be willing to see the faults in our lives so we can make righteous changes.

3. Be Grateful for the Blessings from God

The people complained about the manna situation so much so that God provided a solution: an abundance of meat in the form of quail (so much quail that they would get sick and tired of it, in fact). When the people saw all the quail that covered the ground over thirty-six inches high, instead of giving thanks to the obvious source (the Lord), they focused on their need of hunger being fulfilled. When God blesses us, we often focus on the benefit to ourselves. Rather, our focus should be on giving thanks to the Lord for the blessings in our lives. We should be in awe of His marvelous power, His gracious mercy, and His loving care for us. We live in a blind and unrighteous world, but we must express gratitude for God's abundant blessings.

DRAWING OUT **THOUGHT QUESTIONS**

1. Why were the women, children, and Levites left out of the census taken in Numbers chapter one? _____

   _____

   _____

2. What were the responsibilities of the Levites concerning travel and camp arrangements? _____

   _____

   _____

3. What were the ways God communicated that His presence would be with the people as they traveled? _____

_____

_____

_____

4. Who was this "mixed multitude" or "rabble" in Numbers 11 and what role did they play in the story of God sending quail? _____

_____

_____

_____

5. Was Moses wrong in bringing the burden of Israel to the Lord? What was God's response? _____

_____

_____

_____

LESSON SIXTEEN
SPYING AND DYING
Numbers 13-14

DRAWING OUT **HIGHLIGHTS**

- Moses sends twelve spies to the land of Canaan, one from each tribe
- The spies report that the land is good, but the people and cities are large and strong
- Caleb says the Israelites can conquer the land/its people with God on their side, but the others do not believe it is possible
- Moses, Aaron, and Joshua tell the people that the land is worth taking and with God on their side, they are able to take the land, but the others still do not believe it
- God becomes angry with the people and threatens to destroy them until Moses pleads with God to change His mind
- God punishes the ten remaining spies and the people for their unbelief as none of them are to enter the promised land...their children would enter only after forty more years in the wilderness

DRAWING OUT **CONTEXT**

The Lord instructed Moses to select a leader from each tribe to be used as a spy to investigate the land of Canaan. Moses asked them to bring back a report of the land, the people, the cities, and the terrain, in addition to bringing back some fruit which was in season at the time. After forty days, they returned from their trip [13:1-25]. When it was time to give a report of their findings, they relayed to the people that the land was "flowing with milk and honey" but the inhabitants and the cities there were both large and strong. Caleb suggested they go and take the city, sure they could conquer it. However, the other spies believed the people there were too strong and mighty and that the Israelites were no match for them [13:26-33].

The people then murmured and complained again, stating that they were brought out of Egypt to die in the wilderness. Then Moses, Aaron, and Joshua told the people that the land was too good to pass up and that with God on their side, there was nothing (or people) to fear! The Israelites did not want to hear that and threatened to stone them [14:1-10]. The people rejected and did not place their faith in the Lord, so He became angry with the people and threatened to kill them. But Moses, as in times past, pleaded with God and asked the Lord to be slow to anger, forgiving the people's transgressions against Him [14:11-19].

God agreed to not destroy the people, but because of their continued pattern of unbelief (even after seeing time and time again how God delivered them), He refused to let any of them enter into the land of Canaan except for Caleb and Joshua. God explained that the people's bodies would fall dead in the wilderness and that their children would have to continue to wander in the wilderness for another forty years due to the people's unbelief. All the spies who had returned (save Joshua and Caleb) then died by a plague sent from the Lord [14:20-39].

After all of this, the Israelites then decided they could overtake the people and the land, yet Moses told them they could not because God was not with them, due to their sin. But they didn't care. They went anyway and were killed by the Amalekites and the Canaanites because they disobeyed the Lord [14:40-45].

DRAWING OUT **DEEPER MEANINGS**

Degrees of Faith

Words can have different meanings. To 'know' someone, for example, can mean "to simply be familiar" with someone or it can mean "to have a close relationship" with them and everything in between. The same gamut can be seen in words like 'belief' and 'faith.' All the spies had belief and faith in God – meaning they were confident of His existence. But only two spies had a belief and faith that took them to the next level – to trust in Him and to obey Him. God asked the question, "How long will they refuse to believe in Me, in spite of all the signs I have performed among them?" to Moses in Numbers 14:11. God was asking when their faith and belief were going to step up to the next level in a sense. He knew they believed in His existence, but they had yet to believe that He could do all things and save them from any situation He wanted. However, Joshua and Caleb's faith was already at that level – they were ready to go and conquer the land knowing God was with them. Their faith was pushing them to act. James makes this point in James 2:17 when he says that faith without action (i.e., works) is dead; what good is it? What good is it to know that God is present, but not know He will take care of His people? All the spies had some faith in God, but not all of them had the degree of faith God required. The same went for the Israelites as a whole...time and time again in their history they lacked the faith they needed.

The Influence of Leaders

When God instructed Moses to have spies sent into the land of Canaan, He told Moses to choose a leader ("chief" – ESV; "ruler" – KJV) from each tribe. A leader is one others look up to, respect, and sometimes appoint from among themselves to a position of honor. So when these spies – leaders – returned from their forty day mission and gave their report, what kind of influence would it have had on the people? This was not some "John Doe" from each tribe sent to investigate, but an authority. If the spies as a whole reported that the land could be taken (even with the large cities and inhabitants) do you think the outcome and people's response would have been different? We can only imagine so. But since the authorities reported otherwise, it makes sense for the people to have agreed with their assessment of the situation (even though they shouldn't have). It's been said that "with great power comes great responsibility" and that is certainly true in this case. Elders today have a great responsibility over their flock as leaders, as the ones the people look to for guidance, as authorities. How strong their influence and faith must be! The New Testament even makes mention of this responsibility in the fact that those who teach (i.e., are an authority) will be judged more strictly (James 3:1). To lead is to influence...what an awesome responsibility.

Marveling at Moses' Relationship with God

What a fascinating thing: the fact that Moses could talk to God as a friend, one-on-one (cf. Deut 34:10), and even change His mind. Moses has already done this before, but in a repeat performance, Moses talked God out of again destroying the people because of their disobedience. Of course, God's will would always be accomplished and nothing Moses did or said would change that. But God's plans and motives changed after Moses spoke to Him and His anger subsided. Consider the statements and arguments that Moses made to God in Numbers 14 and reconsider the arguments and the overall communication Moses had with God after the people fashioned their golden calf in Exodus 32. Moses literally was a lifesaver on multiple occasions and had such a unique position and relationship with the Lord.

DRAWING OUT **TAKE AWAYS**

Three things you should remember after reviewing this lesson:

1. Walk by Faith, Not by Sight

The ten spies who saw the land for its large cities and large inhabitants were afraid. They were walking (i.e., living) by sight and not by faith. Their sight told them of their physical situation, but their faith (if they had any) would have reminded them of their spiritual situation – almighty God was with them! Walking by faith is to fear God more than man. Walking by faith is not walking blindly. The spies had seen demonstrations of God's power time after time. Similarly, we too should walk by faith and not by sight. We serve the same God and we too do not have a blind faith; God's word and His creation contain all the evidence we need. When we walk by sight and put fear, importance, or precedence on things in the world (which have no significance in eternity), we are just like the ten spies who did not remember the God they served. Paul tells the Corinthians in 2 Corinthians 6:6f that they are to "walk by faith and not by sight" and the Hebrew writer in Hebrews 11:6 states that without faith – true, obedient faith – we cannot please Him.

2. Christians Are in the Minority

Two out of ten...not a large percentage. That was the number of people who had total faith and belief in God versus those who did not. Just like Joshua and Caleb, faithful Christians are also in the minority in the world, and many times, even amongst those who claim to be believers. Jesus said in Matthew 7:13-23 the way that leads to life is narrow and there are few who find it. There will be many people who don't find their way to the promised land of heaven. One's true faithfulness will shine through when he or she is tested, just as the spies were. But when one's true colors are seen and they become unfaithful, it is even more discouraging to faithful Christians as the number gets seemingly smaller and smaller. Imagine how Joshua and Caleb must have felt when the other spies lost their faith. We do not need to be concerned with numbers, but with being faithful to God (even if we're alone or in the minority) and standing up for what is right. In the Bible we have numerous examples of those who prevailed through their faith in God, even when they were outnumbered or alone. A verse of strength is found in Deuteronomy 20:1 when we "battle" against people of the world and non-believers: "When you go out to battle against your enemies and see horses and chariots and people more numerous than you, do not be afraid of them; for the LORD your God, who brought you up from the land of Egypt, is with you."

3. Realization of Sin is Not Enough

As pointed out previously, we must understand there is a difference between simply coming to a realization of what we did wrong (recognizing it) and determining to change our behavior in an effort to stop the sin (repenting of it). The people had sinned when they lost their faith in God, assuming they could not take the promised land. After Moses pointed out their sin, the people were then fully conscious of it, even admitting it in Numbers 14:40, "...for we have sinned." However, their recognition did not mean they changed their hearts or behavior, because shortly after making this statement, they also claimed they were going to go and take the land...without God. Having God's support was the only way the land could have been taken, but they thought they didn't need God; they thought they had this on their own. However, we see that since they did not truly change, ask for God's support, and wait for Him to be with them, they were killed due to their lack of repentance and for their arrogant attitude. Peter tells the people in Acts 3:19 both to repent and turn to God – that is the way to change and find favor in God's eyes.

DRAWING OUT **THOUGHT QUESTIONS**

1. Imagine God on the mountain looking down at humankind today, could He make the same statement He made in Numbers 14:11? Explain. ___

_____

_____

_____

_____

2. How was the length of time the Israelites had to remain in the wilderness as punishment calculated? _____

_____

_____

_____

3. List as many opposing/opposite traits that Joshua and Caleb possessed versus the remaining ten spies. _____

_____

_____

_____

4. The people committed two sins concerning taking the land of Canaan. The first was unbelief after the initial report. What was their second sin after they changed their minds about taking the land? What can we learn from this today? _____

_____

_____

_____

5. What is ironic about the statement the people make in Numbers 14:2? _____

_____

_____

_____

LESSON SEVENTEEN

KORAH'S REBELLION

Numbers 16-17

DRAWING OUT **HIGHLIGHTS**

- Korah organizes a group to rebel against the leadership of Moses and God's plan
- In response to the rebellion, God opens the earth and swallows Korah and his followers whole
- God makes it clear who He wants serving as high priest by having Aaron's staff bud

DRAWING OUT **CONTEXT**

In Numbers 15, the Lord finishes giving Moses a few additional commands and then we read a story about a Sabbath-breaker. A man was caught gathering sticks on the Sabbath Day, which we know was forbidden. This man was put to death for his crimes and the Lord had tassels placed on the corners of garments to remind the people of the seriousness of the Law. The quick forgetfulness and rebellion of God's rules begin here, because in Number 16-17 there is an organized rebellion against Moses and God's choice in leadership.

Notice the players who took part in the rebellion in Numbers 16. We have Korah, the son of Kohath, the son of Levi. Korah was not a part of the priestly line, the branch of Aaron. As a son of Kohath, Korah would have been responsible for the setting up and breaking down of the Tabernacle, transporting holy items of the Tabernacle, and some teaching of the Law. We also have Dathan, Abiram, and On – all sons of Reuben. The families of

Reuben and Kohath were both living on the south side of the camp, which might explain how they got together in this rebellion.

The conflict of interest started with the selfish attitudes of Korah and his group, who did not approve of the leadership roles God appointed [16:1-2]. They gathered together a group of two hundred fifty leaders, representatives of the congregation, and renown men. The first accusation Korah had against Moses was that Moses exalted himself as holy, when in fact the whole congregation was holy [16:3]. Although God had selected the Israelites to be His set apart people, Korah did not recognize Moses' leadership role in guiding God's people. The Lord, through Moses, clearly illuminated Korah's motivation of self-righteousness and his problem of jealousy [16:4-11]. Moses called these individuals to come out and face him, but they refused and continued offering accusations from their own comfort [16:12-15].

The next morning, Korah and the two hundred fifty followers appeared before the Tabernacle. Moses instructed the people of Israel to step back and separate themselves from Korah and his men [16:16-23]. Moses issued a statement, telling the people that the Lord would make it clear who the Lord sent to be the leader of the people [16:24-30]. After Moses spoke, the Lord opened the earth and swallowed Korah and his followers whole. Then God sent fire up from the earth to destroy the two hundred fifty leaders [16:31-35].

Moses set up a sign for the people to help them remember the events of Korah and who the proper high priests were to be [16:36-40]. After these events took place, some of the people grumbled against Moses because they did not like how God killed their own people. The Lord did not like this grumbling, and sent a plague to destroy those with that attitude. Aaron stepped in, appeased the Lord, and stopped the plague from spreading any further [16:41-50]. The Lord decided to make it even more clear as from where the high priests would come. God told Moses to take a staff from each leader of the tribal houses (twelve total) and include Aaron's name on the staff for Levi. Moses put the staffs into a tent of witness/testimony and removed them the next day. Aaron's staff had budded [17:1-13]. This was a sign to the people that God had made His decision as to who was going to serve Him in this capacity.

DRAWING OUT **DEEPER MEANINGS**

Aaron's Budded Staff

Aaron's staff budding might have seemed like a small sign from God, but it symbolized a very important concept. It is not up to man to decide the ways of God. God had set aside a special group of people to serve Him in the Tabernacle. The staff that budded showed God's divine plan: Aaron's family would be the high priest line. It was important enough that the staff was eventually put into or near the Ark of the Covenant in the Most Holy Place (Heb 9:4; Num 17:10). This sign from God convinced the people that the priests, especially the high priests, had a special place in the nation of Israel. We do not have a budded staff today to remind us of God's organization of His worship. Instead, we have something great and more permanent to remember: His word.

The Earth Opening Up: Miraculous or Natural?

A controversy surrounding Korah's rebellion is the concept of God opening the earth and swallowing people. Skeptics try to find rationale to explain (naturally) the events of Numbers 16. For instance, some suppose that the land of this event was located on a 'kewir,' or an area of land with "a fairly solid crust overlying marsh-like terrain." With the right conditions on the right time of day, individuals could claim that the event could have happened naturally. While this event could have had a natural element to it (although that might be a stretch), it should in no way detract from the supernatural elements attached to it. This event was clearly from the hand of the Lord and a miraculous event that could have only come from God. This was an act of divine judgment (just like the parting of the Red Sea) and not a random seismic phenomenon.

DRAWING OUT **TAKE AWAYS**

Three things you should remember after reviewing this lesson:

1. Rebellion Against Righteousness

Korah accused Moses of being "holier than thou" in his exaltation. In other words, Korah accused Moses of thinking all about himself and being selfish. Why, as readers of Exodus, Leviticus, and Numbers, is this such an absurd accusation? Moses interceded a countless number of times for the people in their arrogance, forgetfulness, and complaints. Moses wanted to see his brethren survive and not suffer the wrath of God, especially during the situation with the golden calf. Instead of a self-righteous ruler, Moses was a humble servant who went to God on the people's behalf. We may meet others who accuse us of having wrong intentions or discourage us from living righteous lives. However, we should not take personal vengeance or revenge into our own hands, but rather look to God for strength, like Moses.

2. The Right High Priest

Aaron's family was designated by God to be the high priest line and this section makes that fact very clear. Likewise, God makes it very clear to us who our high priest is: Christ. The Old Testament high priest was appointed by God and Christ was also appointed by God (Psalm 110:4). The Old Testament high priest offered multiple sacrifices for sins, whereas Christ offered Himself once as a sacrifice for sin (Heb 7:27). The Old Testament high priest sacrifices gave a temporary covering for sins, whereas Christ gave a sacrifice for all sin, completely putting away sins forever (Heb 9:26). One may not like that fact (and one might wish there was another high priest line other than Christ), but Christ is the only true high priest. We can either accept Christ as our high priest or be like Korah and reject God's appointed one!

3. Following the Way of Christ

Korah's rebellion is mentioned in the New Testament book of Jude. Jude warned his brethren about false teachers who had crept in unnoticed, comparing them to a few different events in Jude 11. These false teachers were compared to Cain (a free thinking mindset), Balaam (a spirit of greed and compromise), and Korah (a full scale rebellion and revolt). Jude warned the brethren not to follow in the ways of the false teachers, but to follow in the way of Christ (Jude 17). When we are faced with false teachers and situations where individuals rebel against the Lord's pattern, Jude gives us a few suggestions: build each other up spiritually, pray to God, remember God's love, persevere, and save others depending on the situation (Jude 20-22). When refuting false teaching, it is often times appropriate to show patience by explaining the correct way of God. Other times might require immediate action – "snatching them out of the fire" – before they are drowned in error. Yet, some situations require drastic measures by "showing mercy with fear, hating the garment stained by the flesh" (Jude 23). Following in the paths of error is a serious offense, and we should be careful we are not following in rebellion of God's authority as Korah did.

DRAWING OUT **THOUGHT QUESTIONS**

1. Analyze the accusation made by Korah. Were any parts of his accusation valid?

_____

_____

_____

_____

2. What could have provoked Korah to this extreme point of jealousy? _____

_____

_____

_____

3. What is the point Moses is making in Numbers 16:8-10? _____

_____

_____

_____

4. What are some of the signs in this section that show Moses was God's rightly
appointed leader of the Israelites? _____

_____

_____

_____

5. How can we be guilty, like Korah, of rebelling against God's appointed

leadership? _____

_____

_____

_____

LESSON EIGHTEEN

THE ROCK, SNAKES, AND BATTLES

Numbers 20-21

DRAWING OUT **HIGHLIGHTS**

- The Israelites arrive in Kadesh and complain about their lack of water
- The Lord tells Moses and Aaron to speak to a rock and then water will be provided for the people
- Moses strikes the rock and water comes out for all the people
- Moses and Aaron did not show the Lord to be holy before the people in their actions at the rock, and as punishment, neither enters the promised land
- The Israelites try to pass through Edom, but the king rejects their request
- Aaron dies on Mount Hor and the people mourn his death
- After complaining again, the Lord sends poisonous snakes which injure and kill some of the people
- The people repent of their complaining and the Lord tells Moses to make a bronze snake, that if looked upon by the people, will heal them
- The Lord provides more water for the people via a well in Beer
- The Israelites win battles against the Amorites and the forces of Bashan

DRAWING OUT **CONTEXT**

The Israelites entered Kadesh and noticed there was no food or water. The people complained to Moses and Aaron (again) asking them the same thing they always did: why did you lead us here to die in the wilderness [20:1-5]? Moses and Aaron approached the Lord with the situation and the Lord said that if they would speak to a rock in the midst of the people, He would cause water to pour out of it for the people and their animals. After hearing this, Moses gathered the people, called them rebels, and then asked, "Must we bring water out of this rock for you?" Then he struck the rock twice with his staff and out came water [6-11]. While water was still provided, Moses and Aaron did this in a way that was not pleasing to God. The Lord said because of their lack of trust and not treating God as holy, they would both be punished by not entering the land of Canaan [12f].

The people then attempted to pass through the land of Edom, but after pleading with Edom's king (even stating they would not pass through his fields or drink his water), he refused to allow them to cross his border [14-21]. After coming to Mount Hor, the Lord instructed Moses to go up the mountain with Aaron and his son, place his priestly clothes on his son, and then prepare for Aaron to die. When the people learned of Aaron's death, they mourned for thirty days [22-29].

Not able to pass through Edom, the Israelites found themselves in a barren wilderness again and started complaining. The Lord then sent poisonous snakes which bit and even killed some of the people. Later the people recognized their sin and requested that Moses ask the Lord to forgive them. The Lord told Moses to make a bronze snake, place it on a staff, and if the people looked upon it, they would then be healed [21:1-9].

The Israelites traveled to Beer where the Lord provided water for the people at a well. The people then sang a song of thanksgiving to God for his provision [10-20]. Continuing on their journey, the people did battle (and won) against King Sihon of the Amorites after he refused to allow them to pass through his land. Then the people defeated King Og of Bashan at Edrei and possessed his land [21-35].

DRAWING OUT **DEEPER MEANINGS**

The Sin at the Rock

What was the sin that Moses committed when he struck the rock and out poured water? While there may be debate on what he did wrong, the text reveals several indications and possibilities, and the Psalmist mentions the occasion in Psalm 106:32f when he says, "By the waters of Meribah they angered the Lord, and trouble came to Moses because of them; for they rebelled against the Spirit of God, and rash words came from Moses' lips." Consider the following:

- He was angry – he called God's people "rebels"
- He did not obey God – he struck the rock instead of speaking to it
- He did not honor God – he asked the people why "we" (i.e., Moses and Aaron; no mention of God) must provide water
- He did not fully believe/trust in God – Numbers 20:12 "...you did not believe Me."

It is interesting to note that the Hebrew phrase "did not believe" used in Numbers 20:12 is the same phrase being used in Numbers 14:11 where we read of the account of the ten unfaithful spies. Furthermore, the punishment was the same in both situations; none of them entered the promised land. Whether it was a lack of faith, poorly chosen words or actions, or a combination of both that caused Moses (and Aaron) to stumble, God was not treated as holy and the faith that the Lord expected was not present.

Looking at the Bronze Snake

Why did God have Moses fashion a snake and lift it up for the people to see? Later we notice that Jesus, in the New Testament, compared himself to this lifted snake. However, Jesus was never represented by a snake, so why did He make this comparison? In fact, Jesus was depicted as a lamb (e.g., John 1:29) while Satan was depicted as a snake (e.g., Rev 12:9)! Looking back it's easy to see that the snake represented their sin and, similarly, Jesus took on sin itself (i.e., He represented our sin) and bore sins on the cross. Here, though, the people were to look to the snake not for a representation of what would save them (as there was no power in the snake itself and Jesus had not come yet), but instead as an acknowledgment of their sin. Before the people could be forgiven of their sin, they had to admit it. Looking upon the snake was an acknowledgment to God that they had sinned, were repentant, and were now looking to God for healing. The first step in salvation today (or getting back in God's good graces for the people in Moses' day) is to acknowledge that we are sinners and we need God's help, grace, and mercy. Looking at the bronze snake meant they were confronted with their sin and they admitted it before the Lord.

Wash, Rinse, Repeat

Throughout their history, we have seen the Israelites' continual cycle in terms of their relationship with the Lord: God gives evidence of His power and issues commands, the people agree to God's commands, at the first sign of distress the people lose faith in God and/or reject His commands, God punishes the people, the people repent and turn back to God and prosper...but only for a limited time. This cycle is evident in Numbers 21 where we see the people being punished because of their unfaithfulness. However, after repenting and returning to God's good graces, look what happens at the end of this chapter: they conquer multiple cities with the Lord's help. When the Lord is on their side (i.e., when they are faithful to Him), He is faithful to them in return and we see them prosper, conquer, and take advantage of the promises God made to them. Israel only enjoys victories when they are back on track. This same cycle is seen in more detail and frequency in the book of Judges, where the people continually reject God, then turn back to Him.

DRAWING OUT **TAKE AWAYS**

Three things you should remember after reviewing this lesson:

1. The End Does Not Justify the Means

The Israelites needed water and they got it. Did they care how they got it? Did they care (or even know) that Moses was disobedient in his producing of the water for the people? Moses had to deal with some difficult people... people who time after time questioned God, blamed Moses, and were stubborn. Moses may have had enough and even thought: who cares how or why...just get these people water so they will stop complaining! However, we see that the end does not justify the means. God expects full obedience in everything – even if in disobedience "good" is being done or produced. In 2 Corinthians 5:10, it is made abundantly clear when Paul writes, "For we must all appear before the judgment seat of Christ, so that each of us may receive what is due us for the things done while in the body, whether good or bad." God expected full obedience, trust, and faith from Moses, but in this rare instance, didn't get it. He expects the same from us.

2. Leaders Are People Too

As humans, we place others on pedestals in our minds. We have mentors and those we admire. However, if we esteem those individuals so highly that they become "flawless" in the faith within our minds, then it becomes a dangerous thing. Those being held in this position are "perfect" in every aspect when it comes to following God. Why is this dangerous? Because it cannot be true. No one is perfect. No one is without sin. No one is without problems, temptations, or issues going on in his or her life...even if they are hidden from view. When we esteem leaders and individuals to such a place and then we find out they do/did sin, what a blow that is felt. We might ask ourselves, "If they can't even do the right thing, how am I going to be able to...?" Moses was a respected leader and one who held a very special relationship with the Lord. But, he sinned and was punished. God is not a respecter of persons (cf. 1 Peter 1:17; 4:17f) and we must remember that there is no one immune to sin – not preachers, teachers, elders, deacons, mentors, role models, Moses, Aaron, etc.

3. Look to Jesus for Healing

John 3:14f reads, "Just as Moses lifted up the snake in the wilderness, so the Son of Man must be lifted up, that everyone who believes may have eternal life in Him." Here Jesus himself makes a direct application and parallel between His being lifted up on a cross when He died and the snake being lifted up in the midst of the people. Both must be looked upon (i.e., believed in) for saving. For the people, looking to the snake on Moses' staff meant they acknowledged their wrongdoing and were looking to God for healing and restoration from their wounds. For Christians, looking to the cross acknowledges that we cannot heal our wounds of sin, and through belief and obedience in the one on the cross, we too can be healed and restored. There was no natural cure the Israelites could have turned to for healing. Likewise, there is no natural cure for sin we can turn to for forgiveness. Without looking to Jesus, we will die in sin – just like the people who didn't look upon the snake. Jesus' powerful statement resonated with the people in the first century who were well acquainted with this event from their ancestors' past. What a powerful statement today as we have the accounts of both Jesus' words and the event of the snakes in the wilderness.

DRAWING OUT **THOUGHT QUESTIONS**

1. If Moses was wrong in his actions at the rock, why would God still perform this miracle and allow water to pour out of the rock for the people? _____

_____

_____

_____

2. Moses loses two people in his life in this section (Num 20-21): Aaron and who else? _____

_____

_____

_____

3. What was the significance of Moses removing Aaron's garments and placing them on Aaron's son when on the mountain? _____

_____

_____

_____

4. According to 2 Kings 18, what became of Moses' bronze snake? _____

_____

_____

_____

5. Aaron has passed away. What were some lessons you learned from the events (good and bad) in this man's life? _____

_____

_____

_____

LESSON NINETEEN
BALAAM & BALAK
Numbers 22-25

DRAWING OUT **HIGHLIGHTS**

- Balak enlists the help of a soothsayer, Balaam, to curse God's people
- Balaam endures strange situations and events to learn an important lesson about speaking God's words
- Balaam becomes responsible for bringing fornication into the Israelite camp

DRAWING OUT **CONTEXT**

Numbers 22 opens with a behind-the-scenes look at Moab's reaction to Israel's victory in the previous chapter...it is not a very confident picture. Moab realized how strong and great the Israelites were [22:3]. The king of Moab, Balak, decided the only course of action was to put a curse on God's people. Balak sent some messengers to Balaam (whom we assume was a well-known soothsayer at the time) offering him a job to curse the Israelites [22:5-7]. Balaam told these messengers from Balak that he needed to consult with the Lord before Balaam could give them an answer. What a great thing – Balaam wanted to do what God commanded him to do! The answer God gave Balaam was pretty straightforward: "You shall not go with these people and you shall not put a curse on My people" [22:12]. Balaam told the messengers from Balak, "The Lord will not let me go back with you" [22:13].

Balak was not a king who accepted no for an answer. He sent back messengers to Balaam with a reward that nearly amounted to a "blank check" in hopes that Balaam would reconsider [22:15-17]. Balak was desperate and scared, thinking the only option in dealing with Israel was to get the best soothsayer to curse them. Balaam asked the Lord again if this was His will. God's answer this time was that Balaam could go with them, but only do the things the Lord would tell him to do [22:18-21].

Jumping for joy, Balaam went out with two servants to travel to Balak, king of Moab [22:21]. As he was traveling, Balaam's donkey kept veering off the main path, which resulted in Balaam kicking his donkey a total of three times. Balaam, who was to curse God's people and control their actions, could not control the movement of the donkey he was riding! We, as readers, know that this veering was triggered by an angel of the Lord (who was invisible to Balaam); the donkey was trying to avoid the angel. In a shocking, almost humorous turn of events, the donkey spoke to Balaam asking what he did to deserve these whippings [22:22-29].

The donkey speaking is certainly the most striking part of the story, but notice the humor when Balaam spoke back to the donkey...like it wasn't a big deal! Balaam was determined to get to the king, and nothing (including a stubborn donkey) was going to get in his way [22:30]. Balaam had his eyes fixed on one thing, yet his own donkey had more insight regarding the situation than Balaam himself. If it wasn't for the donkey veering off, the sword of the angel would have cut off Balaam's head, sparing the donkey [22:31-33]. After having his eyes opened, Balaam had a conversation with the angel and acknowledged his wrongdoing. Balaam was reminded that any words he were to speak should only be the words that God would put in his mouth [22:34-35].

The story progresses to its climax with Balaam in front of king Balak having the choice to either curse God's people and receive riches beyond measure, or speak the words God would tell him [22:36-41]. Balak took Balaam to three different places, hoping they would inspire great words of cursings [23:1-24:9]. In reality, God put words of blessings into Balaam's mouth each time so that the king's anger was kindled after the third trip [24:10-12]. God, through Balaam, spoke one last oracle before the king [24:15-25]. This last prophecy actually had some Messianic tones and messages in it, which shows us God was the one behind Balaam's speakings.

We move to a different point of view in chapter twenty-five. We see Israel getting involved in fornicating relationships with the daughters of Moab [25:1-5]. Why did God's people do this and why mention it here in

Numbers? Because Balaam was behind these sinful activities. In Numbers 31:16 we are told, "Behold these [acts with the Midianite women], on Balaam's advice, caused the people of Israel to act treacherously against the Lord." Balaam was not in control of his mouth. Every time he tried to curse God, God took over and provided a blessing instead. However, Balaam was greedy and wanted the money from king Balak. We piece together different sections of scripture to determine that Balaam told Balak how the king could get God to curse His own people – by infiltrating Midianite women into the camp of the Israelites. Balaam found a "back door" to get the money he wanted from king Balak. The events of Numbers 25 were the result of an "indirect curse" from Balaam.

How did God decide to deal with such blatant disregard of His commands? The Lord instructed Moses to kill all of the chiefs of the people and the men who involved themselves in these unlawful relationships [25:3-5]. To further remove the cancer, Phinehas, the high priest's son, stepped in and speared the chief's son and his mistress while in their tent [25:6-18]. By doing this, Phinehas caused God to remove the plague and saved the Israelites from any further wrath.

DRAWING OUT **DEEPER MEANINGS**

"Curse Those Who Curse You"

In Genesis 12:3, God told Abraham and his descendants that He would "bless those who bless you and curse those who curse you." This passage is called to our minds when we read that Balak wanted to curse God's people; we really see a clear testing of God's promise to Abraham. Did God really curse the people? Was God going to let this hot-shot prophet who was batting an impressive .300 curse the Israelites without any repercussions? From what we can tell, Moses and the Israelites did not know the behind-the-scenes details we have recorded for us in Numbers 22-25. It is incredibly faith-building to see that God kept His promises, even when His own people had no clue what was happening. God is an all-knowing, all-seeing, and all-powerful God who does not take lightly those who trample on His holy name.

God's Message is Not Conditional on its Medium

God spoke a lot in this section, although God Himself was not actually the one doing the talking. He spoke His words through different mediums. First, He spoke directly to Balaam, telling him not to curse the Israelites. Then, God spoke through a donkey, helping Balaam learn an important lesson. Finally, God spoke through Balaam himself, putting words into his mouth. By our standards, would the donkey and Balaam be "morally qualified" mouthpieces, mediums, and instruments of the Lord? Clearly not. Yet God can and will use whatever medium He deems necessary to speak His will. We read in Ezekiel and in Jeremiah that God used Nebuchadnezzar, king of Babylon, as an instrument of God's judgment against nations (Jer 27:6). God is not limited as to how He reveals His will. Today, God chooses to reveal His message and will through His word, the Bible. Remember that all scripture is breathed out by God (2 Tim 3:16).

DRAWING OUT **TAKE AWAYS**

Three things you should remember after reviewing this lesson:

1. "Re-Examining" the Commands of God

The first impression we get of Balaam is a positive one; he wants to consult with God first before giving Balak and Moab an answer. But notice the wording of Balaam when he says, "The Lord will not let me go down with you." This sounds like a child who really wants to go out with his friends, but can't because his mommy and daddy won't let him. This is the first sign of something a little fishy in Balaam's attitude and motivation. After a second attempt from Balak to get Balaam to reconsider, Balaam makes a very impressive statement saying, "Though Balak were to give me his house full of silver and gold, I could not go beyond the command of the Lord my God to do less or more." But Balaam immediately goes back and inquires of the Lord, just to make sure the Lord has not changed His mind. Nothing has changed since the last time Balaam and the Lord spoke... except the amount of money. This again shows signs of something a little fishy in Balaam's attitude and motivation. Do we do the same with the Bible today? Often times people "re-examine" the scriptures, hoping to find something different the next time they read them. Why? Let us not use the excuse of "re-examining" the scriptures just to find justification for our sinful actions. Reading God's word should be done with an open heart, with no preconceived motives, in a way that correctly divides the Word of Truth.

2. Learning Lessons from God

God has given us a whole book full of stories with lessons for our learning. The Old Testament is full of stories of a sinful nation and the New Testament is full of stories about a world that either accepts or denies Christ. There are so many lessons to be learned from the Word of God. Balaam learns a big lesson from God, even though he doesn't know it at the time. When the donkey keeps going off the path, Balaam whips him back to the path. This happens a total of three times. Notice what other part of the story involves the number three: chances to curse God in front of King Balak. God intervening with the angel and the donkey is possibly done to teach Balaam an important lesson, one that he needs to learn very quickly. Often times, we have challenges and struggles in our lives. Perhaps God has put us in situations so we can overcome them and become better servants. Whether or not He is directly involved in teaching us a lesson, every time we are faced with a challenge can be an opportunity to learn more about righteous and holy living.

3. Removing the Cancer from the Congregation

The actions of Phinehas are bold. Some argue that he is out of line by killing the chief's son and his Midianite. We clearly see that sin cannot be tolerated within the Lord's congregation. Fortunately for us, we are left with guidelines and principles in an effort to remove the cancer of sin from our local churches. The sad truth is that there are some churches who tolerate sinful acts and individuals in their assembly and church family. By not obeying the words of God, these churches foster an environment where sin spreads like cancer. This story of Phinehas is an incredible example of not allowing blatant sin and rebellion to grow in the Lord's church today. We need to follow the biblical principles of congregational discipline we see laid out for us in the New Testament.

DRAWING OUT **THOUGHT QUESTIONS**

1. Why would Balak ask a prophet of God to curse God's own people? ___

_____

_____

_____

2. What was Balaam's motivation throughout this account? _____

_____

_____

_____

3. Did God change His mind when Balaam approached Him the second time [22:18-22]? Why? _____

_____

_____

_____

4. Why do you think only Balaam's donkey (and not Balaam) could see the angel? _____

_____

_____

_____

5. How did Balaam indirectly "curse" God's people in Numbers 25?

_____

_____

_____

LESSON TWENTY

PREPARING THE PROMISED LAND

Numbers 26-36

DRAWING OUT **HIGHLIGHTS**

- God instructs Moses to take a census of the people
- God selects Joshua to lead the people and succeed Moses
- The Israelites conquer the Midianites in battle
- Reuben and Gad request to stay in Gilead instead of the promised land
- Moses recounts the travels of the people from Egypt to the plains of Moab
- The promised land is divided up, towns created, and cities of refuge established

DRAWING OUT **CONTEXT**

In Numbers 26 God instructed Moses to take a census of the people. Through verse fifty, the individuals of each tribe were numbered and in verse fifty-one the total number of men in Israel equalled 601,730.

At the end of Numbers 27 Moses asked God to appoint a replacement leader for the people, since God had informed Moses that he would not be entering the promised land with them [27:12-17]. The Lord told Moses to take Joshua and bring him before the people, lay hands on him, and commission him [27:18-23].

In Numbers 31 the Israelites became disobedient as they conquered the Midianites. The people decided to allow all the women to live, and when Moses found out about this, he was very upset [31:14]. Moses explained that the women were responsible for enticing the Israelites in the past, and now any woman who had slept with a man must be killed [31:17]. The

Israelites had a great victory over the Midianites, capturing over 675,000 sheep, 72,000 cattle, 61,000 donkeys, and 32,000 virgin women.

In Numbers 32 the tribes of Reuben and Gad inquired of Moses, asking permission to remain in Gilead...they found it fit for their livestock. Although all the people were on their way to the promised land, these two tribes wanted to stay behind. When they approached Moses about this proposal, he became upset and reminded them of when their ancestors also wanted to forgo the promised land and how they were punished for it [32:6-14]. After Moses' rebuke, they changed their request and asked if they could still fight and do whatever it took to get the Israelites to the promised land. They wanted to build pens for their animals, leave their wives and children in Gilead and then return only after the promised land had been conquered [32:16-19]. Moses agreed to their proposal, but warned them if they did not follow through with their commitment (i.e., they don't fight or they come back too soon), they would become sinners and punishment would come. They agreed and the land was given to them [32:31-33].

God told Moses to record the stages of their journey from Egypt all the way to the plains of Moab. So the complete, itemized record of their travels was recorded in Numbers 33.

In Numbers 34-36 the promised land's boundaries were determined, inheritances (i.e., portions of the land) were divided among the tribes, and cities of refuge were established. God instructed towns to be made in which the Levites could live (since they did not get any land inheritance like the other tribes did). All in all, the Levites were awarded forty-eight towns to live in, six of which were to be cities of refuge [35:1-8]. The cities of refuge allowed someone who committed manslaughter (i.e., not premeditated murder) to be safe from their accuser if they remained in the city [35:22-28]. The book of Numbers ends in chapter thirty-six when God told the people that each Israelite's inheritance was to remain within their own tribe; it could not be passed from one tribe to another [36:7-9].

DRAWING OUT **DEEPER MEANINGS**

Drive Out All the Inhabitants

As we read the Bible, God's people and servants continually dealt with outside influences from other nations and people. While the Israelites were to remain holy and set apart from everyone else, sometimes outsiders crept in – people, idols, practices, etc. When the people were at the border of Canaan, God told Moses to tell the people to "Drive out all the inhabitants of the land before you. Destroy all their carved images, all their molten images, and demolish their high places" [Num 33:52]. The last two verses in the chapter explain the consequences if they did not follow the Lord's command. God says, "But if you do not drive out the inhabitants of the land before you, then those whom you allow to remain will be irritants in your eyes and thorns in your side, and will cause you trouble in the land where you will be living. And what I intended to do to them I will do to you." It's clear that God did not want them to have any part of what was in the land of Canaan. The Israelites had already been tempted and led astray with idols (e.g., the golden calf) and with outside women (e.g., the Moabites). God's servants and future leaders fell victim to the same things...all because they did not completely remove these cancers. It's clear to see that God was trying to get the people to completely and utterly replace the bad with good and leave nothing behind that would lead the people away from His goodness.

Cities of Refuge

Six of the forty-eight cities given to the Levites were designated as cities of refuge [Num 35:6ff]. Joshua 20:7f tells us that those cities were Kedesh, Shechem, Hebron, Bezer, Romath, and Golan. Under the Old Law, the punishment for murder was death (Ex 21:14). However, if the killing was unintentional, the killer could go to one of these cities of refuge and find safety from those who wanted to harm him. The killer was safe from harm until his trial, in which the people would decide if the killer acted with any premeditation or not. If the killer was found to have killed unintentionally, he could remain safe in the city of refuge until the death of the high priest, at which point he could return to his home. If the killer left the city of refuge before the death of the high priest, those who wanted to harm him had the right to kill him [Num 35:24-28]. It has been suggested that these cities were among those of the Levites because they would have been impartial as judges due to the fact they were already mediators (between God and the people). The cities themselves could be viewed as a 'type' of Jesus – He is a safe place people can go when they are trying to keep the adversary from attacking them. He is the only true refuge from sin.

DRAWING OUT **TAKE AWAYS**

Three things you should remember after reviewing this lesson:

1. The Journey May Not Be an Easy One

As the people journeyed to the promised land from Egypt, each step is recorded in Numbers 33. What a journey it's been. We have seen ups and downs, victories and defeats, faithfulness and rejection, good and bad... we've seen it all. But, the people finally made it to the promised land just as God said they would. When we look back at our walk with God in our lives – looking at each step along the way – what do we see? Probably much of the same...ups and downs, good and bad. When we look back at our physical lives, we see the same thing as well. All people experience good and bad times, ups and downs, etc. However, Numbers 33 reminds us of all the things the people had to go through and all the lessons they had to learn along the way before they reached their goal. Let this be a lesson to us: getting to the promised land is not easy and living in this world is not easy. There will most likely be ups and downs along the way, both physically and spiritually speaking. But we can always turn to the stories of God's people and find one thing – when they kept their faith in God and obeyed Him, He was always faithful. If we keep our eyes fixed on God and his commands, we too will be able to overcome our ups and downs, look back on our history and possibly say the same thing: although there were many ups and downs, we made it with God's help.

2. Always Yearn for the Promised Land

The tribes of Reuben and Gad saw a land they thought was "good enough" for them and their livestock. They saw benefits in its location and features.

However, they were on their way to what would seem to be a better place – a promised land that would flow with milk and honey. Why would they want to forgo this land? Today, Christians are on their way to a promised land too, but some get comfortable here and find things "good enough"... so much so that they don't have the desire for heaven as they should. While there are benefits and enjoyable aspects of this life, they pale in comparison to what God promises His faithful followers. Let us not give up the fight and get comfortable here, forsaking God and His commands thinking that this life is "good enough" for us and we don't need God in our lives any longer. We must remember that our citizenship is in heaven, not here. Paul makes this point in Philippians 3:20 and 4:1 when he says, "But our citizenship is in heaven. And we eagerly await a Savior from there, the Lord Jesus Christ...Therefore, my brothers and sisters, you whom I love and long for, my joy and crown, stand firm in the Lord in this way, dear friends!"

3. The Impact of Specifics and Record Keeping

As Christians, we are not to have a blind faith in God. Instead, our faith should be based on evidence and truths found inside and outside of God's word. One key aspect to "validating" some of the accounts we read in the Old Testament is specificity. It has to be faith-building to consider the fact that the Old Testament accounts – including the Old Law and stories of Moses and the Israelites – are not some "generic stories" included in the Bible that may or may not be factual. The world wants us to believe that is the case...fictional stories. But, the fact that the Old Testament is filled with specificity and details makes it even more clear that the events contained therein were real-life events. For example, in this lesson we find the exact number of items recovered from the Midianites [Num 31], the exact measurements of the promised land divided among the tribes [Num 34], the record of all the locations the Israelites traveled after leaving Egypt [Num 33], and the number of all the Israelite people via the census [Num 26]. In other places we read of dates, reigns of kings and leaders, dollar amounts, ancestries, and other things that bring specificity to the accounts. These specific records and details may have served a greater purpose in their time, but they are not lost on us today as they continue to have another purpose: faith-building.

DRAWING OUT **THOUGHT QUESTIONS**

1. Why did the Levites not receive any land after entering Canaan? ____

_____

_____

_____

_____

2. What was the reason God gave Moses as to why he could not enter the promised land? Who else was not able to enter for the same reason?

_____

_____

_____

3. What was the Peor incident that Moses refers to in Numbers 31:16? __

_____

_____

_____

4. After reading Numbers 33:50ff, how can we "drive out the inhabitants" in our own lives? How might they "give trouble in the land where you will live" if we do not remove them? _____

_____

_____

_____

5. Besides the specificity and record keeping, what other faith-building features do you find in this lesson's text and in the greater Old Testament? _____

_____

_____

_____

_____

MOSES' LAST SERMON
Deuteronomy 27-30

DRAWING OUT **HIGHLIGHTS**

- Moses gives one last sermon (or set of sermons) to a new generation of people
- God spells out specific curses and blessings that will arise, all dependent upon on the actions of the Israelites
- God reinforces the covenant promise with His people with a specific focus on the land promise He made to Abraham

DRAWING OUT **CONTEXT**

The majority of the book of Deuteronomy is one large sermon (or set of sermons) that Moses preached shortly before his death. Moses tried to encourage obedience and motivation to the Israelites, especially since God's people did not have proper faith when they spied out the land (Deut 1:19-46). While Deuteronomy 1-26 deals with aspects of the Old Law, in this lesson we will start in chapter twenty-seven.

In chapter twenty-seven God reinforced His land promise to Israel and laid out a plan for what would happen when the people crossed the Jordan River. One tribal group was to be placed on Mount Ebal and another group on Mount Gerizim [27:11-14], where blessings and cursings were to be declared. Twelve specific curses are mentioned in Deuteronomy 27:15-26 and are on a variety of subjects. The curses were to be read out loud by the Levites and this reading was fulfilled in Joshua 8:30-35.

After the twelve specific curses were spoken, God told the group of potential blessings and cursings [28:1-68]. These blessings and curses depended on one thing: their faithfulness. Earlier on Mount Sinai, God (through Moses) spoke similar blessings and cursings to the generation that came up out of Egypt (Lev 26). That generation had died and passed away, so God showed His wisdom in repeating these blessings and cursings to the current generation of Israelites on Mount Ebal and Mount Gerizim.

In Deuteronomy 29-30, God spoke words that summarize His covenant with them. God had renewed His covenant with them before and spoke about it, but this time the focus was more specific. This covenant speech dealt primarily with the Israelites keeping the land. If the people were faithful and obeyed the commands of God, they would keep the land He gave them. But if they were unfaithful, they would be driven out of the land.

DRAWING OUT **DEEPER MEANINGS**

The Theme of the Twelve Cursings

While the twelve curses mentioned seem to be random and unrelated, there could be some possibilities that link them together. The nature of their "secret" sins mentioned in Deuteronomy 27:15 and 27:24 is one possible connection. These curses would then serve as a reminder that God sees all things done in secret and that nothing is hidden from Him. Another possibility is that these curses provide motivation for righteous living, as indicated by a response of "amen" after each curse. Often times, negative reinforcement is needed to find motivation to serve the Lord.

A Land Still Flowing with Milk and Honey?

The Bible describes the promised land as a place "flowing with milk and honey" (Ex 33:3). Back in the days of Moses, it certainly was a land that was fertile and valuable. If one looks at the promised land today, however, it looks very desolate and wasteful. Why would a land that was supposed to be fruitful look like it does today? Perhaps the answer is found in Deuteronomy 29:22-29. God says that if the people rebel against Him, the land will be "burned out with brimstone and salt, nothing sown and nothing growing." God was not trying to keep a secret from His people – if they did not keep His commandments, the land would be destroyed. Could the modern day promised land area be a continuation of the promises God made to His people thousands of years ago?

DRAWING OUT **TAKE AWAYS**

Three things you should remember after reviewing this lesson:

1. God Keeps His Word

In discussing the blessings and cursings in chapter twenty-eight, Moses summarized the section by saying, "If you will not obey the voice of the Lord your God...then all these curses shall come upon you and overtake you" [28:15]. The Lord promised His people that certain consequences and blessings would occur if they obeyed/disobeyed. Prophets would often reference these chapters of blessings and cursings. For instance, Elijah predicted a drought in front of Ahab (1 Kings 17:1; Jas 5:17), which calls back to one of the curses mentioned in this section [28:20]. God's people put their trust in Baal for a fruitful harvest and rain, but God is where all men should put their trust. Another example of this is seen in Amos 4:6-11. When God gives consequences for disobedience, He means it. When He gives blessings for obedience, He means it, too. Both of these are manifestations of God's mercy. We can choose to obey or not to obey God, and we have motivation to do His will in the form of both positive and negative reinforcement.

2. God's Expectations Are Not Secret

Notice what God (through Moses) had the people do with His words: set up a monument and shout them to each other [27:2f, 11-26]. The blessings and cursings were to be communicated multiple times and put in various forms. The people could see the large stones and remember God's words. The people could hear each other chanting the curses of God and remember God's words. God gave His people a song to sing in chapter twenty-eight, another reminder of His words. God did not make

His expectations secret to His people. Rather, He made them very clear and communicated them in different ways. When we try to understand God's will and expectations for us, He does not keep the mystery of Christ a secret; His expectations for Godly living in the New Covenant are made perfectly clear to us (Col 1:26). For example, God does not give us just one passage to "figure out" baptism, the Lord's Supper, or church discipline, etc. Instead, the Bible is full of different passages that all communicate to us what the will of God is as a whole.

3. Jesus Christ: Choose Life or Death

The choice God presented to His people was a simple one – serve God and you will live, don't serve God and you will die [30:15f]. Many in the religious world only want to focus on one part of that statement: the life we have in Christ. The tendency is to present the Christian gospel as a life-saving gospel only and forget about the consequences of ignoring it. In fact, many religious leaders adamantly forsake and ignore the pathway of death, claiming that God will not really send millions of people to their spiritual doom. Yet, just like the Old Law, the Law of Christ calls for a choice between life and death. Which pathway are you following? Are you following a pathway of life, described as the narrow way, or a pathway of death, described as the broad way (Matt 7:13)?

DRAWING OUT **THOUGHT QUESTIONS**

1. Why did God speak blessings and cursings to the Israelites, considering He already did so while on Mount Sinai in Leviticus 26? _____

_____

_____

_____

2. God gave His people various ways to remember His promises in Deuteronomy 27. What are some different ways God reminds us of Him and His promises today? _____

_____

_____

_____

3. Has God kept back from us any of His expectations? How do we know? Do we have all that we need to find salvation? _____

_____

_____

_____

4. How is the decision to put on Christ a choice between life and death? Provide scripture(s) to back up your answer. _____

_____

_____

_____

5. According to Deuteronomy 30, where does the word of God dwell? Where in the New Testament is this verse quoted and what is the application there? _____

_____

_____

_____

LESSON TWENTY-TWO
MOSES' SUCCESSOR
Deuteronomy 31-33

DRAWING OUT **HIGHLIGHTS**

- Moses is one hundred twenty years old and prepares the people for his death
- The Lord approves of the new leader, Joshua, while reminding the people the real leader is the Lord Himself
- Moses teaches the congregation a song of the Lord
- Moses gives one last farewell address to the Israelites, blessing the tribes of Israel and asking petitions of God

DRAWING OUT **CONTEXT**

At one hundred twenty years old, Moses prepared the people for his death and the transition of leadership. Moses reminded the people that he was not able to enter the promised land (because of the incident at the rock). As an unsettling thought, the people might have wondered what was going to happen to them now. Moses told the people two things: the Lord is their ultimate leader who will lead them into the land and Joshua will take the place of Moses in the leading of the people [31:1-8]. Moses publicly announced the new leadership of Joshua and gave the people confidence in him.

Moses wrote down the words of the Lord and gave them to the priests. He decided it would be a good idea to have a formal gathering of the people every seven years in which the Law would be publicly read [31:9-13]. By hearing the words of God, the people would learn to fear the Lord and would be careful to follow all the words of the Law [31:12]. The

Lord then spoke to Moses and Joshua in the tent of meeting to fulfill two purposes: to give approval to Joshua as the new leader [31:14-15] and to teach people a lesson in the form of a song [31:16-23]. God was giving the people every possible way to strengthen themselves so they would not rebel and forsake Him. Moses afterwards reinforced this concept to the Levites, encouraging them to continue in steadfastness and righteous living [31:24-29]. Deuteronomy 32 details the song Moses taught the people and Deuteronomy 33 gives Moses' final blessing on the people of Israel.

DRAWING OUT **DEEPER MEANINGS**

God Hiding His Face

God spoke to His people one last time through Moses in the form of a song [31:19-22]. During this song, references were made to the Israelites failing to keep their side of the covenant and their abandonment of God. Was there a benefit to God being this blunt, direct, and negative to the people? God knew the best way to accomplish His purposes. Perhaps the Lord used negative reinforcement to motivate His people, even though God knew what they would do. The imagery in Moses' song shows God "hiding His face" from the people. This phrase is repeated again in Micah 3:4 (talking about a future event) and Ezekiel 39 uses the phrase in the past tense when it says, "The nations will know that the house of Israel went into exile for their iniquity because they acted treacherously against Me, and I hid My face from them; so I gave them into the hand of their adversaries, and all of them fell by the sword" (Ezk 29:23). We can see God took His words and promises seriously in Deuteronomy and He certainly hid His face from the Israelites in Ezekiel! There came a point where open rebellion against God's will was too much.

The Song of Moses

The song recorded in Deuteronomy 32 was most likely the song God taught Moses in Deuteronomy 31:19. This song had a few purposes: to teach the people of Israel, to remind them of God, and to be a witness of the Lord's promises and character [31:19]. The Lord is described as a rock seven different times in this song, which shows the steadfastness and solid dependability of the Lord. While the Lord is reliable, the Israelites are shown as unreliable [32:4f]. Was this the way the Israelites should have repaid the Lord [32:6]? Absolutely not! God chose them, He rescued them, made them His special people, gave them His land, treated them as His pride and joy, and viewed them as the apple of His eye [32:7-13]. Israel was described sarcastically as 'Jeshurun' (a poetic name meaning skinny or upright) because God blessed them so much that the people became fat (which is a good thing). But God's abundance of blessings was not reciprocated by the people, as they scoffed at the Lord during any slight chance of oppression [32:15-17]. What did God do when He saw them scoffing and scorning at Him? He turned His face away from them and let them go [32:18-25]. We see God deliberating with Himself; He would have just annihilated the people for their rebellion, but pagan nations would see God destroying His people as their victory and not God's judgment. God spared His people from total destruction because of His own reputation within the whole world [32:26-35]. The amazing thing is, God still blessed His people [33:36-43]! It is easier for us to understand God's judgment and wrath than His grace because Israel deserved wrath and not grace. Amazingly, God will still bless His people and curse their enemies. This song should remind the people of God's blessings, the seriousness in keeping the Law, the wrath of God when they do not keep His words, and His grace that abounds even more.

Moses' Final Blessing

Before the Israelites moved into the promised land, Moses took the opportunity to remind them of a few things. First, Moses recapped what the Lord had done for them and His greatness that appeared to them [33:1-5]. The Lord was their king who appeared on His "throne" on Mount Sinai. Moses then gave blessings and petitions to God on behalf of the tribes of Israel (except Simeon, probably because it was to be scattered and absorbed by Judah). Reuben was the oldest son, but his blessing was short and did not get a lot of attention in the text [33:6]. Judah was next, where Moses asked the Lord to help them have success in battle [33:7]. Why this petition? Judah was the tribe that was going to lead the people into battle. Of Levi, Moses spoke of their great acts of faith in Exodus 32, where they defended the Lord during the golden calf incident

[33:8-11]. The idea of the Urim and Thummim was that the Levites had their resources to inquire of God (cf. 1 Sam 14:41f). Moses petitioned the Lord for protection against any adversaries of the Levites. The next tribe was Benjamin, where Moses asked for security and safety of God [33:12]. Joseph was mentioned next, but there was never a tribe of Joseph. Why? Joseph was to receive a double portion as the firstborn of Rachel (Gen 48:5) so his sons, Manasseh and Ephraim, became tribes [33:13-17]. Moses turned his attention next to Zebulun and Issachar, brother tribes who were often mentioned together in a pair. Moses blessed them to find success in their sacrifices and living [33:18f]. Of Gad, Moses mentioned them getting the land first and of their enlarging borders [33:20f]. Moses' statement of Dan and Naphtali was short, with petitions that they find success in conquering the land [33:22f]. Finally, Moses mentioned Asher, where oil would anoint the people's feet and the bars (of their gates) would be like iron...symbolizing blessings of wealth and strength [33:24f]. Why talk about all of this? These blessings and petitions on behalf of the Israelites show us they had all the reason to be happy, secure, and safe in the arms of God [33:28-29].

DRAWING OUT **TAKE AWAYS**

Three things you should remember after reviewing this lesson:

1. Be Strong and Courageous

Imagine how the people of Israel felt knowing their leader, since the Exodus, was no longer going to be with them. Moses was about to leave, but he reminded the people that it did not matter! Although Moses himself would no longer go with them, the Lord God would go before them. The Lord would destroy their enemies (give them into the Israelites' hands) and lead them to the promised land. It was at this point that Moses said, "Be strong and courageous. Do not fear or be in dread of them for it is the Lord your God who goes with you!" (Deut 31:6). The people did not need to focus on the fact that Moses was not with them, but instead needed to focus on God being with them. It really does not matter whom God uses, but rather that God is with us. The way we can be strong and courageous is to have the Lord as our leader and put our complete trust and faith in Him. In every work we do for the Lord, the only factor that ultimately matters is knowing God is with us.

2. Be a Generation That Knows the Word

In one of his last acts as the leader of the Israelites, Moses commissioned a special memorial service (a reading of the Law) every seventh year during the Feast of Booths. Did Moses need to do this? We know that the Law was to be taught by the Levites to the congregation and that parents were to bind the Law on their children's hearts. Certainly the people studied the Law and read it more than once every seven years, but the symbol was that each and every generation should know God's word. Moses wanted the people to keep this special day so that each generation after him had absolutely no excuse in not knowing the Law. This might even be what Ezra did when he read the book of the Law to the people in Nehemiah 8:1-8. We are a generation blessed so much more beyond previous generations. We have Bibles everywhere – on our phones, in our homes, in bookstores, in libraries, etc. We have study materials that other generations did not have. We have the internet, which provides resources of online sermons, bible studies, articles, and other helpful information. There is no excuse for not knowing – even almost having memorized – the word of God! Let's make sure we are not guilty of being a generation that does not know the Word of God.

3. God's Promises Provide Joy

In Deuteronomy 33:27-29, we see a powerful statement that summarizes God's past, present, and future for His people: "The eternal God is your dwelling place, and underneath are the everlasting arms. And He thrust out the enemy before you and said, 'destroy.' So Israel lived in safety, Jacob lived alone, in a land of grain and wine, whose heavens drop down dew. Happy are you, O Israel! Who is like you, a people saved by the Lord, the shield of your help, and the sword of your triumph! Your enemies shall come fawning to you, and you shall tread upon their backs." Moses reminded the Israelites what the Lord had done and the care He provided for them; God was keeping His promises! Moses said that this fact should provide happiness and joy to the people, because God had saved and rescued them. God is described as their shield of help and their sword of triumph. God has made certain promises to us today, specifically that He will supply our every spiritual need (Phil 4:19). These promises provide us great joy and help us get through the darkness of this life.

DRAWING OUT **THOUGHT QUESTIONS**

1. How did Moses express concern for the people in his "farewell address?"

_____

_____

_____

_____

2. What are some ways (like what Moses instituted) that we can implant God's law in the hearts of our descendants/children? _____

_____

_____

_____

3. Why is the song Moses taught the people full of warnings regarding disobedience? How would that motivate God's people to serve Him?

_____

_____

_____

4. Moses set up a new "holiday" which the people were to celebrate every seven years. Give reasons for or against Moses' right to set up a special day. Do we do the same today? Gives reasons for or against our right to set up special holidays. _____

_____

_____

_____

5. What are some promises that God has made to you in the New Testament and how do they give you joy? _____

_____

_____

_____

MOSES' DEATH

Deuteronomy 34-Joshua 1

DRAWING OUT **HIGHLIGHTS**

- Moses ascends to Mount Nebo where God shows him the promised land
- Moses dies in the land of Moab at one hundred twenty years old
- The people weep and mourn Moses' death for thirty days
- Joshua becomes the next appointed leader of the Israelites
- The people agree to obey Joshua, just as they had Moses
- Joshua prepares the people to enter the promised land

DRAWING OUT **CONTEXT**

Moses went up to Mount Nebo and there the Lord showed him all the promised land that was sworn to Abraham, Isaac, and Jacob's descendants. While Moses could look at the land, God did not allow him to enter the land. Moses died in Moab and was buried in the valley. He was one hundred twenty years old. For thirty days the people wept and mourned over the loss of their leader [34:1-8]. The text says that Moses was unlike any other prophet in Israel, in multiple facets [34:10-12].

Moses had earlier laid hands on Joshua, appointing him to be the next commander and leader of the people. God then formally commissioned Joshua, explaining how He will be with Joshua (just as He was with Moses). God reminded Joshua over and over again to be "strong and courageous" as the people were about to take over and receive their promised land. Joshua commanded the people, prepared them for what was to come, and the people responded with, "Just as we obeyed Moses in all things, so we will obey you" [Joshua 1].

DRAWING OUT **DEEPER MEANINGS**

The Impact of Moses

The fact that the people mourned and wept over Moses' death for thirty days shows the impact he had on them. No other prophet would be like Moses and the people's loss was a great one. Consider the impact Moses also had within the New Testament – he's mentioned in numerous places. He appeared with Elijah and Jesus at the Transfiguration (Matt 17:3f; Mark 9:4f; Luke 9:30, 33), the Hebrew writer mentioned him in the "hall of faith" in Hebrews 11:24-29, and even John made mention of Moses and his song in the book of Revelation (15:3). Certainly this man not only had an impact on his contemporaries, but on those who would read and learn about him centuries later.

Laying Hands on Joshua

Deuteronomy 34:9 states that Moses "laid his hands" on Joshua and then the people listened to Joshua. Numbers 27:18-23 also provides the account where Moses was told to "lay his hand upon [Joshua]." This physical manifestation was to show Moses' (i.e., God's) approval of Joshua. The Israelites fully understood this because the people obeyed and followed Joshua after his anointing. The laying on of hands is seen even into the New Testament and simply provides a gesture authenticating a person with a spiritual gift, healing, duty, ability, or appointment (cf. Acts 6:1-6; 8:14-22; 13:1-3). The laying on of hands had no power in and of itself, but was used as a sign to witnesses and to the appointed individual.

DRAWING OUT **TAKE AWAYS**

Three things you should remember after reviewing this lesson:

1. Moses Wrote About Jesus

There have been many connections made to Moses as a foreshadowing and 'type' of Jesus. It's also important to note that while parallels can be made between Moses and Jesus, Moses actually wrote about Jesus.

Several passages indicate this:
- Jesus shows references to himself in the Law of Moses – Luke 24:44
- Philip says that Moses wrote about Jesus – John 1:45
- Jesus says Moses wrote about Him – John 5:46
- Moses predicts Jesus – Acts 26:22
- Paul taught Jesus from the Law of Moses – Acts 28:23

Clearly this shows God's overall plan – which He knew from the beginning – in that the Old Law was temporary (as was Moses), but later a New Law and a new prophet would come to usher in the era of the church and last forever. It is fascinating to contemplate how much Moses knew of what he was actually writing (i.e., the prophetic nature of it) during his time on earth, and that his writings would be used in the first century and beyond in the teaching of the gospel.

2. Leaders Should be Respected

The people had come to respect Moses as their long-time leader, but now that Moses had passed, it was time for a new leader. Sometimes we don't like new leaders, new bosses...change in general. Hebrews 13:17 says, "Obey your leaders and submit to them, for they are keeping watch over your souls, as those who will have to give an account..." While not referring to Moses or Joshua, the Hebrew writer states that even today we are to respect those who are leaders in the church because they watch over our souls. Were not Moses and Joshua to do the same – watch over the people and ensure they were always being faithful to God? Leaders in such positions are to be respected – no matter who they are – because of the great responsibility they have to watch over their people. In the time of Moses, Joshua was divinely appointed to be their leader and Paul told the first century Christians that God was the one who established some positions of leadership, even outside the church (cf. Rom 13:1), and as such, those positions should be respected. The Israelites obeyed and respected Joshua from the very beginning when they proclaimed, "Just as we obeyed Moses in all things, so we will obey you." May this too be our attitude to those in leadership roles today.

3. God Keeps His Promises

The people finally made it to the promised land. Through a number of events including their disobedience, punishments, and repentance, they had reached the land that God had promised them. The people questioned many times if this day would actually come, or if they were simply led into the wilderness to die. But God is faithful. Peter, in one of his sermons, made the point that in addition to a promised land, God promised a savior and He also delivered on that promise in Jesus – "From the offspring of this man [David], according to promise, God has brought to Israel a Savior, Jesus" (Acts 13:23). He will also deliver on His promise of eternally punishing the wicked and rewarding the faithful on the day of judgement (cf. John 12:48; Rom 12:19; Matt 24:36). How can one not believe this is the case when we see God keeping all of His promises – in His own time – throughout history? When we think to question when Jesus will return (or, God forbid, we question if that will actually happen and live unfaithfully) we should remember the Israelites who waited (probably a lot longer than they expected), questioned the same things and became unfaithful at times...yet God was faithful to the end.

DRAWING OUT **THOUGHT QUESTIONS**

1. Why was Moses not allowed to enter the promised land with his

   people? _____

   _____

   _____

   _____

2. What was one of the first things Joshua led the people through that is

   reminiscent of what Moses did early on in his leadership? _____

   _____

   _____

   _____

3. How long did it actually take the Israelites to reach the promised land after leaving Egypt? Why? _____

_____

_____

_____

4. What did it mean for Joshua to be "strong and courageous" as God instructed him to be multiple times? How can we be strong and courageous today? _____

_____

_____

_____

5. List the thing(s) that impacted you most or that was gained from studying Moses, the person. _____

_____

_____

_____

LESSON TWENTY-FOUR

OUT WITH THE OLD, IN WITH THE NEW

DRAWING OUT **HIGHLIGHTS**

- The Old Law served a purpose in God's overall plan for mankind, but is inferior to the New Law
- The New Law ushers in the opportunity for all of mankind to be saved from sin and allows non-Jews to be among God's people
- Jesus' death is the one event that instituted/started the New Law, while at the same time "nailing the Old Law to the cross"
- Under the New Law, God still expects His commands to be followed with the proper heart, spirit, and in full obedience

DRAWING OUT **CONTEXT**

As we've just reviewed in the first twenty-three lessons, by God's infinite wisdom and knowledge, He saved a group of people from bondage, made them His own, entered into a covenant with them, and provided for their needs. Although through the Old Law alone one could not be saved, God knew a better, new law would be ushered in through the death of His Son that would offer salvation for all mankind – before and after Jesus' death on the cross – to those who were/are obedient to Him. Some may question the purpose of a law that was "not good enough" and would have to eventually be replaced. The Bible makes it clear that God had many purposes for the Old Law:

- It showed God's holiness to the people (Deut 5:22-28)
- It defined sin to the people (Rom 7:7, 13; 1 Tim 1:9; Jas 1:22-25)
- It showed God had selected Israel as His people (Psalm 147:19f; Eph 2:11-17)

- It provided the standard of Godly living for the people (Deut 4:1; 5:29; Jud 2:19-21)
- It eventually prepared the Israelites for God's son (Gal 3:23-4:7)

While the Old Law served many purposes during its time, it was inferior to the New Law Christ introduced due to one main aspect: it did not provide salvation. Indeed, the Old Law was never put in place to be the "end all" to the problem of sin. This fact is seen in passages such as Hebrews 10:1-4 (cf. Acts 13:38f; Rom 3:20). The Bible indicates that the Old Law was also inferior in other areas:

- To be justified under the law, it had to be kept perfectly...but that was impossible; only Jesus kept the law flawlessly (Gal 3:10-13; Rom 3:10, 23; Heb 4:15)
- The law could not perfect anything (Heb 7:11-19; 10:1f)
- The law could not make one righteous (Gal 2:21)

Since the New Law has been ushered in, Christians are no longer bound to the Old Law. The New Testament makes it abundantly clear that the Old Law is no longer binding in Romans 6:14, 7:1-6, Galatians 5:1-4, 18. Chapters eight, nine, and ten of the book of Hebrews show that the New Law is superior to the Law of Moses in several regards, including the fact that Jesus was the one-time sacrifice offered for all mankind.

Although a new law is in place, it still contains the same principles and many of the same commands that we see in the Old Law. In fact, all of the Ten Commandments except for remembering the Sabbath Day are mentioned elsewhere in the New Testament, making it clear that other commandments are still binding.

The New Law might have brought about a change in the method and ability to be saved and justified in God's eyes, but there has not been a change in what God expects from His people: full obedience. While many surmise the New Testament in the single word 'grace' and others the Old Testament in the single word 'obedience,' it is important to remember that from the very beginning God always expected full obedience (including today under the New Law) and He has always extended grace and mercy to His people (including under the Old Law). It is incorrect to claim that it was only under the Law of Moses that God expected obedience and He lacked giving grace and mercy to His people, just as it is incorrect to claim that today God doesn't expect full obedience assuming His grace and mercy suffice.

What a blessing it is to know that from the beginning, through the man Moses and the giving of the Old Law, and then through the man Jesus and the institution of the New Law, God had a plan to save mankind from sin!

DRAWING OUT **DEEPER MEANINGS**

Can Christians Ignore the Old Testament?

What's the point of studying an outdated, defunct law originally written for another group of people? Can Christians simply ignore the Old Law because it is no longer applicable? Certainly not. Several passages indicate how Christians can benefit from the Old Law even today. First, the Old Law was written to teach and encourage us (Rom 15:4). Second, it helps us see the need to focus on God, holy living and conduct, instead of on worldly/ sinful things (1 Cor 10:6, 11). Third, we learn from the principles found in the Old Law and make current-day applications (Gal 5:13-26). While we are not under the Old Law, ignoring it completely would be to lose details about who God is (i.e., His holiness, personality, etc.), how His people should act, how the New Testament writers relate the New Law to the Old, and how we can fully understand the entirety of God's plan of salvation.

Seeing the Old Law in the New

All but one of the Ten Commandments are repeated in the New Law and in several places within the New Testament. Lest one think that these "old" commandments are no longer binding, below is a list of the Ten Commandments (minus the Sabbath Day observance) seen again in the New Testament which shows their reinstatement (i.e., bindingness) in the New Law:

1. Have no other gods before God (Acts 14:15; John 4:21-23;
   1 Tim 2:5; Jas 2:19)
2. Have no idols or images (Acts 17:29; Rom 1:22f; 1 John 5:21;
   1 Cor 10:7,14)
3. Do not take God's name in vain (Jas 5:12; Matt 5:33-37, 6:5-9)
4. Honor father and mother (Eph 6:1-4)
5. Do not murder (1 John 3:15; Matt 5:21f)
6. Do not commit adultery (Matt 5:27f; 1 Cor 5:1-13, 6:9-20; Heb 13:4)
7. Do not steal (Eph 4:28; 2 Thess 3:10-12; Jas 5:1-4)
8. Do not lie (Col 3:9; Eph 4:25)
9. Do not covet (Eph 5:3; Luke 12:15-21)

DRAWING OUT **TAKE AWAYS**

Three things you should remember after reviewing this lesson:

1. Obedience and Grace

Is it true God cares about obedience only in the Old Testament and cares about grace only in the New Testament? This is a dangerous and incorrect understanding of the differences between the two covenants. God was always concerned with the heart in the Old Covenant, as indicated by God's statement of "bind these words of Mine in your hearts" (Deut 11:18). We also see in Isaiah that God did not accept sacrifices from His people anymore because they were offered with vain hearts (Isa 1:11-14). God cared about both His commands and the hearts of the people in the Old Testament. What about the New Testament? The book of Romans (a book that discusses grace in detail) begins and ends with a discussion on the obedience of faith and not a discussion on unconditional election (Rom 1:5-8; 16:19, 25-27). Paul tells us that being free and alive in the spirit means that we keep in step with the spirit, practicing fruitful acts (Gal 5:13-26). We have been offered eternal life because of God's grace and our multitude of sins will be remembered no more. But does that mean we should "continue in sin so that grace may abound?" Paul says in Romans 6:1, "By no means!" We have been saved through grace through the shed blood of Jesus, but to come into contact with that blood/grace signifies there are works involved (Heb 9:11-28). Other passages that talk about obedience and grace include Galatians 6:2, Matthew 7:21, James 1:22, 2:14-26, and 1 Peter 2:7f.

2. Commands or Byproducts vs. Commands and Byproducts

Was it more important for the Jews to obey God or simply to change their hearts? What about us today? Should we be more concerned about obeying the will of God or just transforming our hearts? There are various false teachings that claim such things as "...the person who already has mercy, justice, faith, and love fulfills the principle and does not need a law to tell him how much of his resources to use in accomplishing these. He is free from lawful requirements because he has the principles (that the laws were to inspire) already written on his heart" (C. Hook, *Free in Christ*). While God certainly wanted His people to change their hearts, that did not nullify any of His commands that would inspire/lead one to a changed heart. A perfect example of this is Nadab and Abihu, who wanted to sacrifice to God but did not do so correctly (Lev 10:1-4). Their hearts may have been in the right place and they may have offered a sacrifice with right motives, but they did not follow the exact commands of God. We cannot love God and have our hearts fixated on Him if we do not keep His commandments. A command and any of its byproducts go hand-in-hand; a person should not have one without the other. Loving God (which can be a byproduct itself) means to keep His commandments (John 14:23). It is a fallacy to think we can be found favorable in God's eyes and gain any byproducts without obeying His commands. Why is this important? As an example today, there is not a way to achieve the byproduct of forgiveness of sins without doing something first. Cleansing our sins with the blood of Christ can only be accomplished through God's plan of action (i.e. His commands) for us.

Change...it's imminent. We've seen in this book: people change, people's zeal and nature change, God's laws change, God's dealings with people change...but there is one thing that is forever unchanged – God himself. God is the same yesterday, today, and forever. Jesus, likewise, is also the same yesterday, today, and forever because He is God. God doesn't change, but that does not mean the way He dealt with mankind didn't change. We know God dealt with Adam and Eve in one way and He dealt with the Jews in another. He now deals with Christians through a new plan/covenant. But God himself – His attributes and His promises – are unchanging. Hebrews 13:8 reads, "Jesus Christ is the same yesterday and today and forever." And in Malachi 3:6 the Lord says, "For I the Lord do not change..." The concept of an unchanging God is also reflected in the very name He told Moses to call Him at the burning bush: "I am." In present-tense, "I am" means now; not was...not later. Without reference to the past or future, this shows that God is the same and unchanging for all time. What a blessing it is to know that we serve the same God as the people under the Old Law, and because He is unchanging, we can learn all about Him from our studies in these books out of the Old Testament.

DRAWING OUT **THOUGHT QUESTIONS**

1. What are some passages that show God is concerned about both obedience and one's heart in the Old Testament? _____

_____

_____

_____

2. What are some other principles, applications, etc. from the Old Law that are also seen in the New Law (outside of the restating of the nine commandments already listed above)? _____

_____

_____

_____

3. How do we know exactly when the Old Law was concluded and the New Law was then under effect? _____

_____

_____

_____

4. While we know that no one could keep the Old Law perfectly (except Jesus), would it be possible for someone to keep the New Law perfectly? Support your answer with scripture(s). _____

_____

_____

_____

5. What are some ways in which you have grown and/or what aspects of the Old Law have you found to be helpful after this study? ___

_____

_____

_____

Made in the USA
Columbia, SC
17 February 2024

31729892R00096